STALINGRAD

STALINGRAD

THE BATTLE THAT SHATTERED HITLER'S DREAM OF WORLD DOMINATION

RUPERT MATTHEWS

ARCTURUS

This edition published in 2014 by Arcturus Publishing Limited
26/27 Bickels Yard, 151–153 Bermondsey Street,
London SE1 3HA

AD003885EN

Printed in the UK

CONTENTS

INTRODUCTION

The vast bloodletting at Stalingrad brought death, injury and misery on an unprecedented scale. Men, women and children were butchered by the hundreds of thousands in conditions of such abject awfulness that even today nobody can say to the nearest 10,000 how many were killed. The human cost was enormous, the horror was unimaginable and the scale of destruction was awesome.

The battle was a disaster for almost everyone involved, but it was Adolf Hitler who came out of it worst. His plans for the conquest of the Soviet Union were destroyed at Stalingrad. Along with them went the Nazis' ambitions for a New World Order. Maps of the Great German Reich had already been drawn up and architects' schemes for the new German cities had been finalized, but they were never to be used. Everything had depended on the destruction of the Soviet Red Army, and at Stalingrad the Red Army showed that it was not about to be destroyed any time soon.

If Hitler had failed to win the war in the west during the Battle of Britain, it's equally clear he lost the war in the east at Stalingrad.

And yet it should never have been like that. Stalingrad was never a key objective of the German army – it was only ever a secondary target. Nor did the Red Army rate Stalingrad as being of any great importance. It was just one of a score of industrial cities in the Soviet Union. Others like it changed hands during the fighting without undue loss to either side. The names of those other cities have largely been forgotten outside their immediate area, but Stalingrad came to be the focus of a titanic military battle of unprecedented proportions, one which decided the fates of entire nations.

This book is about why this city became so important and the effect this had on the lives of those caught up in the terrifying conflict.

1
A WORLD AT WAR

The Second World War began with a German attack on Poland early on 1 September 1939. With hindsight we know that the German–Polish War would spread to engulf the entire world and would drag on for six long, bloody years. But at the time things did not look like that. The man who had started the war and who would greatly influence the conduct of the Battle of Stalingrad certainly had no such knowledge or intentions.

Hitler's vaulting ambition

Adolf Hitler invaded Poland with definite plans in mind, none of which involved Stalingrad. Hitler's immediate aims were to restore to Germany the borders that she had enjoyed until the crushing defeat of 1918. Large areas of western Poland had until 1918 been part of Germany. Parts, but by no means all, of those areas had large populations of Germans, which only added to Hitler's determination to bring these lands under the rule of his Third Reich.

The annexation of western Poland was intended to be only a part of the general reorganization of Eastern Europe that Hitler had in mind. Of course, that reorganization was to be entirely to the benefit of Germany so far as Hitler was concerned, but he was enough of a realist to know that he would have to deal with the ambitions, views and priorities of the other states involved. Lurking at the back of his mind throughout these years was the more distant prospect of reorganizing the Soviet Union to the benefit of Germany as well.

German politics during the 1920s had seen the Nazi Party pitched into outright and often violent opposition to the Communists. Now that the German Communists had been crushed, the Nazis could see no reason why they should not continue to view foreign Communists as the ultimate enemy. Since the Soviet Union was the only Communist state in the world at this date, its eventual destruction featured consistently, though not always prominently, in Nazi propaganda and ambitions. Not only was the Soviet Union controlled by Communists, but it was also populated by Slavonic peoples. In Nazi ideology, Slavs were '*Untermenschen*': that is, second-grade humans who were fit only to be treated as slaves for the benefit of the superior Germans.

Although there is no doubt that Hitler and many Nazis held such views, it is equally clear that in 1939 a trial of strength with the Communist Slavs was seen as something of a distant prospect. Such a struggle would no doubt come one day, but not yet.

Of rather more immediate concern was the fact that Britain and France had in March 1939 agreed a military alliance with Poland. If Hitler invaded Poland, he now knew that Germany would be at war with France and Britain as well. The alliance had come as a surprise to Hitler, who had been convinced that neither France nor Britain would go to war over events in Eastern Europe.

The march into Prague

In 1938, Hitler backed a Nazi coup in Austria that led to Austria joining with Germany. Later in 1938, Hitler threatened to invade Czechoslovakia if the Sudetenland, a border area with a German-speaking population, was not handed over to Germany. As an act of appeasement, Britain and France signed the Munich Agreement, which complied with Hitler's demands.

In March 1939 German diplomacy scored a huge success. For some months the Germans had been talking to politicians of the Slovak People's Party, led by Jozef Tiso. The Slovaks had for generations been wanting independence from the old Habsburg Empire and in 1919 had been none too pleased to be pushed into the new state of Czechoslovakia, especially as they were outnumbered by the Czechs. The Germans now egged on Tiso, promising him German trade treaties and military advisers if the Slovaks declared themselves independent of Czechoslovakia.

On 14 March 1939 a meeting of Slovak parliamentarians announced their withdrawal from the Czechoslovak parliament and the independence of Slovakia. On the same day the head of the Czech Nazi Party issued a public call for German troops to enter the Czech lands to 'restore order'. In marched the German troops and the Czech lands became the Protectorate of Bohemia and Moravia, under German military rule.

Hitler had also been making strenuous diplomatic efforts to woo Admiral Miklós Horthy, ruler of Hungary. Strictly speaking, Horthy had been Regent for the absent King Charles IV, but Charles had died some years earlier. However, the Hungarian parliament had confirmed Horthy in his powers as Regent. The far eastern end of Czechoslovakia, Ruthenia, had a largely Ukrainian and Hungarian population. By pre-arrangement with Hitler and Tiso, Hungarian troops marched into Ruthenia to annex the province on the same day that the Germans entered Prague.

Even Poland had got in on the act. When Tiso announced Slovak independence, President Ignacy Mosciki declared his support for the move, then sent Polish troops to annex the city of Teschen (now Cieszyn) before the Germans could get there.

Non-Aggression Pact

Czechoslovakia had been carved up after careful German diplomacy and naked threats of military action. Poland was to be next, so the sudden interference of France and Britain came as a shock.

Hitler, however, was not dismayed. It seems likely that he had originally planned to follow the pattern set in Czechoslovakia by combining diplomacy, threats and promises to achieve the destruction of Poland to Germany's benefit.

Now, backed by France and Britain, the Poles shrugged off German threats and diplomacy and became truculently defiant, so Hitler decided to resort to open war for the first time in his career. He knew that Poland had to be defeated quickly so that neither France nor Britain would be able to do anything to help.

But if Poland was to be invaded, Hitler had first to ensure that none of the countries bordering Poland would interfere. To the south lay Slovakia and Hungary, both now in Germany's debt after the dismemberment of Czechoslovakia and unlikely to help the Poles. East of Hungary lay Romania, which also shared a border with Poland. Germany's relationship with Romania was more complex. Romania had fought against Germany and the Habsburgs during the First World War and in the Versailles Treaty had been rewarded with extensive lands that had belonged to the Habsburg Empire, as well as some lands that had formerly been part of the Russian Empire. As a result, King Carol eyed the rise of Hitler's Germany warily. On the other hand, the Romanian oilfields around Ploesti were a major source of oil for Germany. Hitler knew that in the event of war against Britain the Royal Navy would soon cut off oil imports from outside Europe, leaving Germany dependent on Romanian oil. He was therefore careful to avoid antagonizing King Carol, though secret help was sent to the Fascist party inside Romania.

To the northeast of Poland was Lithuania, but with a population of only 2.5 million it could safely be ignored. What could not be ignored was the mighty Soviet Union, which bordered Poland to the east. If Germany were to annex all of Poland, the result would be a long and vulnerable Soviet–German border. Moreover, Soviet dictator Stalin would most likely see such a step as a belligerent move against Russia and might begin preparations to attack Germany in a pre-emptive strike. Hitler might well have intended to invade Russia at some point years into the future, but 1939 was not the time. Fortunately for him, Hitler knew enough history to see a way to get Stalin on his side.

If western Poland had been formed out of lands formerly belonging to Germany, eastern Poland was mostly made up of lands that had belonged to Tsarist Russia before 1918. In 1919, the incumbent Soviet leader Lenin sought to recover those lost provinces, and spread

Soviet Communism, by invading Poland. The Poles annihilated the Russian invaders, then launched their own counter-invasion that swept deep into Russia. The resulting Treaty of Riga saw Poland acquire large areas of Russia. The Soviet commander whose army had been defeated in the later stages of the war had been one Josef Stalin, now ruler of Soviet Russia. Hitler correctly judged that Stalin was eager for revenge.

German diplomatic moves began in April 1939 and reached fruition in August, with the German–Soviet Non-Aggression Pact. Ostensibly the new treaty was one of friendship, with trade and commercial aspects. Among other things, it pledged the two states to remain neutral if the other went to war and set out a complex commercial deal by which Russian grain, oil and metal ores were swapped for German cars, trucks and other manufactured goods. That was only the facade, designed to fool outsiders.

The treaty also included secret clauses that stipulated how much of Eastern Europe would be carved up between Germany and Russia. Poland was to be invaded by Germany, which would annex the western half. As a gift for allowing this, Russia would be given the eastern provinces lost 20 years earlier. Stalin would have his revenge on the Poles. In addition, Germany pledged diplomatic support for Russia in its border dispute with Romania over the province of Bessarabia. Not only that but other countries were also to fall under the 'sphere of influence' of Germany or Russia. Germany would get Lithuania, while Russia would get Finland and Latvia. Quite what form this 'influence' would take was left unclear. The Germans seem to have interpreted it to mean something similar to the relations they currently enjoyed with Slovakia and Hungary. Stalin had other ideas.

Blitzkrieg in Poland

With all of the countries bordering Poland now supportive, Hitler turned to his military men. Over the previous ten years or so, the German military had been developing a revolutionary new concept of warfare that would become known as 'blitzkrieg', or 'lightning war'. While most other armies were planning for long, drawn-out wars of attrition fought from static defensive lines, as in 1914–18, the Germans were planning a fast-moving war of manoeuvre. The key weapons of blitzkrieg were to be the tank, or panzer (short for *Panzerkampfwagen* – armoured fighting vehicle), and aircraft, both equipped with radio to enable swift and effective communications with each other and with high command. Working together, the panzers and the bombers would break through the enemy front lines while the fighters gained and kept control of the air above. Once through the enemy defences, the panzers would race ahead to penetrate far and fast, disrupting enemy reinforcements, destroying command and control centres and grabbing key strategic points. The bombers would meanwhile bomb any enemy forces they could find, and could be called up by the panzers to pound any intact defences the panzers could not destroy. The infantry, meanwhile, would be marching up as fast as they could, in order to exploit the confusion caused by the panzer–bomber partnership.

On 1 September 1939 Hitler unleashed the German blitzkrieg on Poland. It worked to perfection. The Poles had positioned their armies close to their borders, hoping to use their light troops to fight a long delaying action in the marshes and forests while the French and British mobilized to invade Germany from the west. It was not to be. The German panzers punched through the borders, then raced along the main roads to capture the towns and cities where the bulk of the population lived. The *Luftwaffe* (air force), meanwhile, bombed the Polish supply system into oblivion so that those troops seeking to stage a fighting retreat soon ran out of food and ammunition. It was all over in three weeks. About 100,000 Polish soldiers marched over the border into Romania, where they hoped to find sanctuary.

The Russians, as agreed, had marched into eastern Poland once they were assured of a German victory. Poland was then carved up between the Germans and the Soviets. Those areas of Poland that had been German before 1918 were annexed to Germany and those that had been Russian were divided into two. The eastern areas were annexed to the Soviet Union while the rest were organized into what was termed the General Government of Poland. Ostensibly the General Government was run by Poles, retaining Polish currency, Polish postage stamps, Polish police forces and so forth – but in reality the area was under German military occupation and Nazi Party officials were installed to give the orders. Both the Soviets and the Germans settled down to impose a harsh, murderous rule on their newly-acquired territories, where they stripped the lands of anything valuable.

Finland fights back

The German armed forces, meanwhile, turned west. The French had begun a half-hearted campaign across the Franco-German border, but this was halted as soon as news of the Polish defeat arrived. On 6 October Hitler announced that Germany wanted peace, but he made it clear that he had no intention of pulling out of Poland. France and Britain refused his overtures, but made no aggressive moves. The Western Front stagnated into what has become known as the Phoney War.

If things were going quiet in the west, they were not so in the east. On 5 October 1939 the Soviets invited Finland to send a delegation to Moscow to discuss unspecified matters of mutual interest. When the Finns arrived they were presented with a list of demands and were told that if they did not agree there would be war. The Soviets wanted to be given extensive lands around Karelia in southern Finland and several islands in the Baltic Sea, and demanded that the Finnish army demolish a number of fortresses that had been recently constructed to defend the Finnish capital of Helsinki from Russian attack. After the Finnish delegation had hurried home to report, the Finnish government offered to cede some border territory to Russia, but they did not give the Soviets everything they wanted. On 30 November the Red Army swarmed over the border into Finland.

The day after the invasion, a group of Finnish Communists announced that they were forming a new Finnish government – though it was clearly a mere front for Soviet occupation. The Finnish army of 337,000 men was outnumbered three to one but the odds were even worse than they appeared, because the Soviets fielded 2,514 tanks to the Finns' 32 and 3,880 aircraft to the Finns' 114.

To everyone's surprise, including their own, the Finns halted the Soviet offensive in its tracks. The landscape favoured defence, while the Soviet army proved to be poorly organized, badly led and ineptly supplied. The Finns, on the other hand, were well trained and well supplied. Their ski troops in particular performed well, using their speed over snow to ambush small Soviet units or melt away from larger ones. By Christmas the Soviets had lost tens of thousands of men but had achieved little. Stalin was furious. He sacked the generals and poured more resources into the war.

A new offensive, launched on 1 February 1940, finally broke through the Finnish defences, but the Soviets were depressed to find that the Finns merely fell back to a second line of defences. Unknown to the Soviets, however, the Finns were almost out of ammunition and trained men. At this point the Swedes stepped in to broker a deal. The peace treaty gave the Soviets everything they had demanded in the previous October, and more than 300,000 Finns became refugees. The Finns, however, congratulated themselves on retaining their status as an independent state and on having inflicted so much damage on the Russians that they would be unlikely to attack again in a hurry.

Hitler had been watching the war with interest. His pact had allotted Finland to the Soviets' sphere of influence so he had no quarrel with Stalin's annexation of Karelia. What did interest Hitler very much, though, was the poor performance of the Red Army. He had known that the Red Army was huge but poorly equipped, but now it seemed that it was badly trained and organized as well.

The Great Purge

This did not come as much of a surprise to Hitler and the German military, since they had heard much about the ruthless purges that Stalin had inflicted on the Soviet government and armed forces in the 1930s. Known collectively as the Great Purge, they had begun in 1936 when Stalin had moved to destroy rivals within the Communist Party. First to go were Grigory Zinoviev and Lev Kamenev, former close associates of Lenin who Stalin feared as rivals. The net gradually widened to include anyone who had shown insufficient loyalty to Stalin or who had ever expressed support for others. By 1938 local party bosses were using the pretext of rooting out anti-Stalin activists to pay off old scores and get rid of their own rivals. In all about 680,000 people were executed, with another million or so imprisoned and vast numbers of others ousted from their jobs and positions. The purge of the Red Army removed 3 out of 5 marshals, 13 out of 15 army commanders, 8 out of 9 admirals, 50 out of 57 army corps commanders and 154 out of 186 division commanders. The lower ranks were not so badly affected, but around 10 per cent of all army officers were removed by execution, imprisonment or reduction to the ranks. The effect of the purges on morale and military capability had clearly been enormous.

Soviet expansion

In May 1940 the long-anticipated German blitzkrieg into France began. The German offensive was as overwhelmingly successful as it had been in Poland. The British army was driven back to the sea, managing to evacuate via Dunkirk, but the French army was utterly destroyed. France surrendered on 22 June. Hitler was jubilant, but events in the east would soon take the shine off his achievements.

On 16 June, as Hitler ecstatically watched his panzers enter Paris, Stalin launched his own campaign of conquest. At dawn an unknown marksman fired a few shots at a Soviet customs post on the border with Latvia. The shots were undoubtedly the work of the Soviet secret service, the NKVD (People's Commissariat for Internal Affairs), but Stalin announced that it was an unprovoked attack by Latvian extremists. The Soviets presented a note to the Latvian government containing demands that would effectively make the country a province of the Soviet Union. Identical notes were given to Estonia and Lithuania, although even according to Stalin's version of events they were not involved. By noon vast numbers of the Red Army were massed on the borders.

All three governments gave in and the Soviets swarmed over the frontiers. It soon became obvious that Stalin was going further even than his notes had demanded. The three Baltic States had a ruthless Communist regime imposed on them, and thousands were taken away for imprisonment or summary execution. Stalin gave ethnic Germans the option of leaving for Germany if they wanted, and tens of thousands took the opportunity to get out. Soon eastern Germany was filled with refugees needing homes, jobs and emergency aid.

Hitler was furious and felt deeply betrayed by Stalin. The Non-Aggression Pact of 1939 had given Estonia and Latvia over to be within Russia's 'sphere of influence', but Hitler had taken this to mean that the states would merely be bullied into accepting Soviet military bases, unfavourable trade agreements and the like. Annexation had not, the Germans thought, been on the cards. In any case, Lithuania had been allocated to the German sphere of influence, but Stalin had annexed it all the same.

The treatment of the Baltic States was bad, but even worse was to follow. Unknown to outsiders the Red Army was being sent south by rail from the Baltic States to the Black Sea. On 26 June 1940 the Red Army appeared on the northeastern border of Romania. In Moscow the Romanian ambassador was given a note by the Soviet government. The note demanded that Bessarabia, that part of Romania that had been part of the Tsarist Empire, be restored to Russia. In addition, the note said, Romania had to hand over the northern half of Bukovina by way of compensation. The note gave King Carol and his government just 24 hours to respond before the tanks rolled in. There was little Romania could do except give in. By nightfall on 28 June Stalin was in control of his new territories.

This new move by Stalin was much more serious for Hitler. The move into Bessarabia might be understood as a desire to restore the pre-1919 borders of Russia, but the advance into Bukovina had no such justification. What it did do, however, was put Russian bombers within flying range of the oilfields around Ploesti. Hitler could see no reason for the annexation of Bukovina other than to mount a threat to the oilfields. It might have been that Stalin had plans for Romania, but any threat to the Ploesti oilfields was a threat to the German economy and to Germany's ability to wage war. Hitler was worried.

Hitler's peace offer to Britain

Worried he might have been, but he was still at war in the west. France had surrendered, but Britain had not. Hitler set about trying to lure Britain to the peace table. His first move was to give France what he considered to be very lenient terms. The border provinces of Alsace and Lorraine were annexed back to Germany, which had owned them prior to 1919, but otherwise

France was left intact and was even allowed to keep its overseas colonies. The French armed forces had to hand over their aircraft and tanks, but the navy was left unscathed and forces in the colonies could retain their aircraft and tanks. Only parts of France were to be occupied by German troops and that occupation was to end as soon as Britain stopped the war. Later the German occupation of France would be extended to the entire country and would become increasingly repressive and bloody, but in the summer of 1940 it was occupation with a light touch.

Then Hitler made a speech in which he made it clear that Britain could expect similarly generous terms. What he wanted, Hitler said, was an end to a war that he had never really desired in the first place, and he was willing to be generous to get that peace. The British government was not deceived. They knew that Hitler was determined to control the entire European continent and was running a brutally repressive regime. There could be no lasting peace with Hitler. The war went on. On 16 July Hitler gave the orders for the invasion of Britain at the earliest opportunity. There then followed the Battle of Britain during which the *Luftwaffe* failed to gain control of the air over the English Channel and southern England. The German navy refused to set out with an invasion fleet until air control was assured and so the invasion was called off for the winter.

Border worries

Meanwhile, Hitler had on 29 July ordered General Alfred Jodl, head of operations at the OKW (*Oberkommando der Wehrmacht* or German General Staff), to prepare plans for how Germany should react should the Soviets attack the Ploesti oilfields. Jodl reported that the main problem was geography. Germany did not share a border with Romania, so the German army could not simply march to aid the Romanians. The best route was via the Hungarian railway system, but there was no guarantee that Hungary would allow the Germans access. The best Jodl could come up with was to suggest that the Germans invade Russia through what had been Poland, then wheel south to attack the flank of the Russian armies invading Romania.

Hitler responded by ordering 12 divisions, two of them panzer divisions, to be sent to the Russian border in occupied Poland. But Hitler made it clear that he did not want to provoke a war. 'These regroupings must not create the impression in Russia that we are preparing for an offensive in the East,' he wrote to Jodl. 'On the other hand Russia should draw the conclusion that we are ready to protect our interests, particularly in the Balkans, with strong forces against Russian aggression.'

The moves by Russia had implications further south. King Boris of Bulgaria had so far sought to stay out of entanglements with countries to his north. The Bulgarians' main focus was on staying on good terms with Greece and Turkey. All trade to and from Bulgaria had to leave either by sea through the Turkish-controlled Bosphorus or overland via the Greek port of Alexandroupolis. The fact that Alexandroupolis had been Bulgarian until 1919 rankled somewhat in

Bulgaria, but ambitions to regain it were secondary to policies aimed at sustained economic growth. But the aggressive moves by Russia made King Boris nervous. While his diplomats in Russia tried to find out what Stalin's ultimate ambitions were, he sent a team to Germany to open talks with Hitler.

Further south still, Greece was in rather more serious trouble. The extensive Greek merchant fleet in the Mediterranean found itself caught in the middle of the naval war between the Italians and the British. Several Greek ships were sunk, mostly by the Italians who mistook them for British ships. In October the Greek cruiser *Helle* was torpedoed by Italian bombers. Tensions came to a head on 28 October 1940 when Italy declared war on Greece and invaded from Albania (then part of Italy). The invasion soon became bogged down as winter weather closed in on the mountains, but the outbreak of hostilities made King Boris of Bulgaria even more worried about the future.

Also worried were the Yugoslavs. By annexing Austria, Germany had gained a border with Yugoslavia.

King Peter was only 17 years old and the Regent, Prince Paul, was proving to be both popular and competent. Hitler had made some diplomatic efforts at retaining Yugoslav friendship, but it had never been a key consideration. Now he found Prince Paul much more enthusiastic than before for the friendship of Germany and Italy, although the Yugoslav Parliament was seriously divided over the issue.

First steps towards Barbarossa

Back in the west, the plans for the invasion of Britain were called off in September. The OKW was told to prepare to invade Britain in the spring, but soon other plans were being pushed forward. The *Luftwaffe* suggested that Britain could be bombed to the negotiating table and proposed the construction of large numbers of heavy bombers to pound the island. The German navy, on the other hand, suggested that Britain could be starved into surrender if the convoy routes could be cut, and proposed the construction of hundreds of U-boats to achieve this end. Debates raged in the OKW as to which plan to follow.

Then in early October 1940 the German intelligence services reported that Soviet newspapers and magazines published for the Red Army had begun printing anti-German stories and were attacking the Nazis and Germany in strident terms. It was suggested that the propaganda was preparing the Red Army soldiers for a possible war with Germany.

Towards the end of the year Sir Stafford Cripps, a British Labour MP, led a delegation to Moscow. Hitler assumed, rightly, that the talks had included secret sessions about the war against Germany and Stalin's attitude to it. Cripps came away empty-handed, but Hitler suspected that Stalin had pledged to support Britain. Hitler believed that Britain would inevitably be beaten by Germany – whether by invasion, bombing or starvation – and could not understand why Churchill had not opened negotiations for peace. Now he thought he had the answer. Britain was holding on because Soviet Russia was going to join the war by launching a surprise invasion of Germany.

Hitler asked Jodl at the OKW to draw up plans for an invasion of Russia. The OKW regularly drew up or revised contingency plans for all sorts of eventualities, no matter how unlikely, so the request did not at first surprise the German military. Jodl gave the task to a brilliantly clever staff officer named Friedrich Paulus. By early November, Paulus had come up with several different scenarios and had begun testing them in war games.

Meanwhile, Soviet Foreign Minister Vyacheslav Molotov paid a formal visit to Berlin starting on 10 November. The talks did not go well. Molotov made it clear that Russian expansion in the Balkans was not yet over and the Germans made it clear that they did not like the fact. In the end, an agreement was reached that neither Germany nor Russia would do anything much in the Balkans for the next few years, but Hitler no longer trusted Stalin. He was convinced that Russia would act as soon as Stalin thought he could get away with it.

On 5 December Jodl took the results of Paulus's thinking and war games to Hitler. The plans were based on the latest intelligence reports. These stated that the Soviets had 100 divisions in existence, and could mobilize another 100 within six months. These numbers were far greater than the German army could muster, but it was considered that the German forces were better trained, better equipped and better led than the Soviets. The debacle of the Soviet invasion of Finland had proved as much. Even so it was recommended that Germany should seek additional troops from its allies. The main fighting would be done by the top-quality German units, but the allies could undertake secondary duties.

Paulus said that the games had suggested two feasible methods of invasion. In the first, more conventional, scenario the Germans would seek to defeat the Soviet army in a series of large-scale battles in western Russia. Once the Red Army had been destroyed, peace could be imposed. A second, more radical, option was for panzer columns backed by infantry riding in trucks to race ahead of the main German army. They would drive hundreds of miles to seize key strategic points, disrupting the Soviet system and so dislocating the Red Army that it would be unable to fight.

Hitler studied the plans, then on 18 December he issued Führer Directive No. 21 – Operation Barbarossa. The invasion of Russia would take place in the summer of 1941. Reaction from the senior military men who were informed of the decision was mixed. Some were aghast at the prospect of attacking the Soviet Union, with its huge resources of manpower and raw materials, while others welcomed the move, believing that the German army was at a peak of effectiveness whereas the Russians were disorganized. Most of them worried about attacking Russia before Britain had been subdued. All of them endlessly debated the merits of the two schemes drawn up by Paulus.

Hitler chose to go with the more conventional invasion model, with the aim of defeating the Red Army in a series of massive battles in western Russia. Many German generals, especially those experienced in panzer units, disagreed. They thought that Russia was so large that only swift, deep penetrations stood a chance of dislocating the Soviet war machine and so ensuring a quick and complete victory. Seeking to defeat the Red Army in conventional battles, they argued, risked the war becoming a war of attrition that Germany could not win. Hitler was unmoved. His decision stood.

Hitler had also accepted the need for allies. Three allies could easily be counted upon. Italy was already Germany's partner in the war against Britain and it would not take much to persuade Italian dictator Benito Mussolini to provide troops for the new conflict. Romania was eager to recover Bessarabia and northern Bukovina, while Finland was even more enthusiastic about any scheme to regain Karelia.

In addition, Hitler had decided that while Britain could be safely kept on the defensive by a combination of bombing raids and naval attacks on convoys, the situation in the Balkans had to be sorted out. Greece would need to be crushed. That meant sending German troops to help the Italians. Hitler won over King Boris by promising him the return of Alexandroupolis in return for German troops being able to use Bulgarian railways and roads to reach Greece. Prince Paul of Yugoslavia was likewise persuaded to allow the Germans free movement through Yugoslavia in return for pledges of German and Italian friendship.

By 25 March everything was ready. Greece would be invaded on 6 April, with total victory to be achieved within three weeks. The invasion of the Soviet Union would then take place in mid-May.

Just two days later things began to go wrong.

2
OPERATION BARBAROSSA

On 27 March 1941 news arrived in Berlin that a coup was under way in Yugoslavia. It was not at first apparent who had launched the coup, nor if it would be successful, but Hitler did at least know that the uprising had nothing to do with him. He suspected Stalin was at work again.

Invasion of the Balkans

When firm news from Yugoslavia came through it became clear that Stalin, like Hitler, had also been taken by surprise. The coup had, in fact, been mounted by a small group of Yugoslav Air Force officers who had long opposed Prince Paul. They had been outraged by the new agreement with Italy and Germany. After ousting Prince Paul, the officers declared young King Peter to be of age and then appealed to the people, who flooded into the streets in support of the coup. It later transpired that the British had been encouraging opposition to Paul and the new pact, though whether they had wanted to risk a coup was never clear.

Hitler reacted swiftly. He ordered the OKW to include the conquest of Yugoslavia in its plans for the invasion of Greece. This required large numbers of additional troops, which in turn meant delaying the invasion of Russia from May to June. Hitler agreed to the delay and the invasion went ahead. Yugoslavia was conquered in 12 days, Greece in 21 days.

A territorial carve-up carefully orchestrated by Berlin then followed. Most of Greece was occupied by the Italians, who annexed several islands and some border territory. Bulgaria took Thrace and the all-important port of Alexandroupolis. Yugoslavia was divided up, with Bulgaria taking Macedonia and Italy gaining Dalmatia, Montenegro and most of Slovenia. Croatia was set up as an independent republic under a pro-Nazi regime. Serbia was likewise independent, but only nominally because it was occupied by the Germans.

Anticipating easy victory

A few German troops were left in the Balkans, but most moved north back to their start lines for the invasion of Russia. Now that Operation Barbarossa was so close, Hitler risked the possibility that news might leak to the Russians by trying to recruit more allies. King Boris of Bulgaria was asked to join the war, but he refused on the grounds that his people had been helped by the Russians against the Turks many times in the past and would not support the move. Instead he offered to send men to drive supply trucks and carry out other duties out of the firing line. He also ordered the arrest of all Communist Party members in Bulgaria.

In Hungary, Admiral Horthy was rather more amenable to joining the war against Russia. The recent advances by the Soviets had given Hungary a border with Russia for the first time in its history, and neither Horthy nor his people liked the fact. Hitler promised that Russia would be pushed back away from the Hungarian border and that Hungary would get a share of the victory spoils. Horthy agreed to declare war on Russia, but sent only a small part of the Hungarian army. In all, three infantry divisions, two mechanized brigades and a cavalry brigade marched east.

After some final reorganization of military units, Hitler ordered that the invasion was to take place on 22 June. This was some five weeks after the original start date, the delay having been caused by the excursion to Yugoslavia and Greece. The delay would prove to be crucial and would lead to the battle for Stalingrad.

The invasion force was divided into three main army groups, each tasked with its own particular mission. Army Group North was composed of the 16th Army and the 18th Army (both infantry units), together with the 4th Panzer Group under General Erich Hoepner.

It was commanded by Field Marshal Wilhelm von Leeb, a veteran artillery officer with anti-Nazi political views. His task was to sweep northeast from East Prussia to destroy the large Red Army concentration in the Baltic States and to destroy the Soviet naval bases on the Baltic coast, thus rendering the Soviet navy useless.

The main bulk of the invasion force was placed in Army Group Centre under Field Marshal Fedor von Bock. This formation comprised the 4th Army and the 9th Army (both infantry and made up of three, not the usual two, corps) plus the elite 2nd and 3rd Panzer Groups. The 2nd Panzer Group was commanded by Heinz Guderian and the 3rd by Hermann Hoth, the two most talented panzer generals in the German army. Together with Bock, Hoth and Guderian had argued for the deep-penetration method of invading Russia and had been deeply disappointed by Hitler's decision to go for a more conventional plan. The tensions would rise again as the campaign unfolded. Several SS (*Schutzstaffel*) units were included in Army Group Centre. It was expected that Army Group Centre would meet the main force of the Red Army, so it was tasked with destroying it.

Army Group South fell under the command of Field Marshal Gerd von Rundstedt, whose task was to destroy the Soviet armies in Ukraine. He had the 6th Army, 11th Army, 17th Army and 1st Panzer Group at his disposal, plus the Romanian, Italian and Hungarian contributions to the invasion. The Romanian commanders were understandably anxious to grab the lands promised to Romania by Hitler, but were reluctant to go much further.

Amidst all of this military planning, the Germans had neglected one of their traditional strengths – propaganda. Moves into Austria, Czechoslovakia, Poland, Denmark, Norway and France had all been preceded by careful analysis of the domestic situation, followed up by sophisticated propaganda campaigns. In each case the Germans had accurately identified those sections of society that might give in quickly, or even collaborate, and those that would fight tenaciously. The stories that were fed to journalists and newsreels were carefully crafted to appeal to the different segments of society, and the messages were usually subtle and effective.

But in tackling Russia, the Germans did none of these things. The huge unrest over forced collectivization among the peasants in the western areas was ignored. The grievances of ethnic minorities were ignored. The bitter feud between the Orthodox Church and Stalin's government went unexploited. Even the demoralized state of the Red Army officer corps after Stalin's purges was never exploited and was barely noticed. German diplomats had sent all of this information to Berlin, but it had been ignored.

The fault for this was largely Hitler's. 'We have only to kick the front door in and the whole rotten edifice will collapse,' he had declared. Added to the Nazi doctrine that the inhabitants of Russia were subhuman, this belief seems to have dominated planning and to have led many Germans to expect a relatively easy military victory. The opening stages of the campaign did seem to justify this belief.

The bulk of the Red Army was stationed in the west, close to the borders of the Soviet Union. Its troops were, therefore, within range of the German strike and would be tumbled into battle before they had time to reorganize. Compared with the German army the Red Army was poorly trained and badly led, but it had comparable equipment and plentiful supplies of both men and munitions. Events would prove that many of the supposedly frontline units in place in June 1941 were supplied with older equipment, but that those mobilized during 1941 would enter battle with the very latest weaponry.

Perhaps the biggest deficiency in the Red Army was an adherence to old-fashioned tactics and strategies. The Soviet forces had barely learned the lessons of the First World War and had not even noticed the advances in armoured and airborne warfare that the Germans had perfected and other nations were scrambling to adopt. The Red Army had always won its victories by the sheer weight of numbers, fighting against adversaries using similar tactics but with fewer men. The Finns, for example, had given the Russians a nasty shock, but had been defeated by overwhelming numbers. Having always won victories with its existing tactics, the Red Army saw no need to change.

The invasion begins

The Germans, Hungarians, Italians and Romanians invaded at dawn on 22 June. In the north, Leeb began a spectacular drive northeast from East Prussia. Hoepner's panzers pushed on ahead and by 26 June were at Daugavpils, while the infantry toiled on behind. As the Germans marched through the Baltic States they were greeted as liberators by the Lithuanians, Latvians and Estonians, who had so recently been taken over by Stalin's Soviets. On 25 June a series of Soviet counterattacks were made around Pskov, but these were beaten back and on 30 June Leeb was on the move again. By 14 July Leeb had achieved his objectives of capturing the Soviet naval bases and destroying the Red Army along the Baltic. His men were tired and his equipment was in need of maintenance, so he called a halt.

In the centre, where it was expected that the main battles would be fought, Bock had drawn up plans for his panzers to penetrate deeply into Soviet territory in two columns, which would then wheel inwards, thus trapping the Russian forces. The infantry would then come up from behind to crush the trapped Russian forces against the panzers, as a hammer smashes an object on an anvil. Two key problems were the mighty fortresses at Brest-Litovsk and Grodno. The panzers dealt with both impediments by simply ignoring them and pushing on east, leaving them to be dealt with by artillery and infantry. By the dawn of 23 June the panzers were 64 kilometres (40 miles) into enemy territory and driving fast.

But even as the panzers raced east, the Germans

gradually began to realize that this campaign was not going to be like previous ones. In other countries, enemy units that had been surrounded and had no hope of rescue had very quickly sought surrender terms. In Russia this did not happen – the isolated Russian troops fought on until they ran out of food, ammunition or both. Brest-Litovsk, for instance, did not surrender until 30 June, even though it had been cut off and was being pounded by heavy artillery. The importance of this difference was quickly made clear to the panzer commanders.

Supplies were brought up on lorries that had road wheels, not cross-country tracks like the tanks. This meant that there had to be a continuous road route in German hands if the panzers were to get their fuel and ammunition. In Russia only a very limited number of roads and bridges were able to carry heavy lorries, because most were designed and built for horses and carts.

All of these good roads went through towns, and it was in the towns that the Russian soldiers took refuge from the marauding panzers. Ordinarily the German infantry and artillery would have bombarded or starved the defenders out, but with the panzer commanders demanding that the roads be opened up immediately the towns had to be assaulted. German casualties began to rise just as the panzers began to be slowed down. This slowing effect was masked in the early days by the rapidity of the Germans' advance and the spectacular victories they were winning. Only the more senior commanders knew that the advance was not as rapid, nor the victories as great, as had been planned.

On the second day of the war, the Germans captured Grodno and reached Kobryn, 64 kilometres (40 miles) from their start lines. The Russians around Bialystok were already in danger of being surrounded. The Soviets pushed their tanks forward to counter the panzers, but while the panzers operated in large groups of units linked by radio the Russian tanks were organized into a host of small units, operating alone. They were picked off piecemeal and destroyed. At Slonim the marching German infantry surrounded two Russian armies and forced their surrender, though thousands of Russians managed to escape in small groups.

On 30 June the panzers captured the great city of Minsk, while the leading units reached the banks of the River Berezina 145 kilometres (90 miles) farther on and 483 kilometres (300 miles) from the pre-war border. Now was the time for the panzer groups to wheel inwards to surround the Soviets. But it began to rain and to rain heavily. The roads around Minsk were made of packed sand, with only one highway surfaced with tarmac. When drenched by rains, the sand roads became soft and unable to take the weight of the German lorries. Within hours the entire German army shuddered to a halt. When the rains stopped and the sun came out the free-draining sand dried out quickly and the army could move again, but several hours had been lost. More time was lost every time it rained, and it rained a lot that summer.

By the time the panzer pincers closed, around 300,000 Russian prisoners had been captured, but at least half a million had got away. Those Russian defenders were now on the east bank of the Berezina and were being joined by new reinforcements, as thousands of reserves were mobilized and units were brought up from elsewhere in the Soviet Union.

Leeb decided that if he had at first failed to destroy the Red Army with his panzer pincers around Minsk, then he would succeed a second time. A fresh offensive was hurriedly planned that would repeat the objectives of the first. The panzers would move forward in two columns again, to destroy the Red Army around Smolensk. There was a delay while the infantry came up – marching 32 kilometres (20 miles) a day for two and a half weeks had made the men understandably tired. Then the new offensive was launched. Guderian chafed at the delay, but was made to wait.

On 12 July Guderian and Hoth were let loose again. Within a day they had broken through the new Russian front line and were heading east at speed to close the trap at Smolensk. Then the rain showers came again, inflicting a series of short but crucial delays on the panzers. Guderian covered 160 kilometres (100 miles) in seven days, but Hoth was slower because he had to cross several swollen rivers.

By this time the Russians were not only getting better organized, but having seen the Germans' manoeuvre at Minsk they also had a shrewd idea of what Hoth and Guderian were trying to do. Marshal Semyon Timoshenko, in command of the Soviet West Front (the Russian equivalent of a German Army Group), hurriedly pushed units into the route he expected Guderian and Hoth to take. The Germans acted as Timoshenko had expected and his new dispositions slowed the German advance. German officer Rudolf Schmidt was riding in a truck accompanying a unit of panzers when it encountered a battery of Timoshenko's anti-tank guns.

'We had just turned a bend when a hail of machine-gun fire greeted us. At first it came only from the left of the road, but we had just begun to take up position when all hell broke loose from the right,

and then from our rear. The Russian fire became so intense that we had to run for our lives and I got into a ditch. Then anti-tank guns opened up and we could see we had run into a tight corner. Before we had regained our breath every one of our tanks had been shot to pieces. Then the Russians began firing into the ditch where we were. It was impossible for us to stay. We had to crawl away on our stomachs. After a few hundred yards of this we got up and found our next unit advancing.'

Although the Russians were unable to stop the panzers, they slowed them down long enough for about a million men to escape the closing trap – leaving some 350,000 men to march into captivity by 5 August.

Unlike Leeb, Bock had not achieved his war aims. The Red Army in front of him was battered, but not yet crushed. He was, however, some 400 kilometres (250 miles) further into Russia than he had originally intended. His supply lines were long and overstretched, his men were tired and his equipment needed attention. Like Leeb he called a halt. Guderian and Hoth were bitterly disappointed. They felt that their original idea of pushing fast and deep into Russia with their panzers but without waiting for the infantry had been the right one. Given their way, they would have been in Moscow by now.

In the south, Rundstedt was opposed by greatly superior Soviet forces, but they were led by one of the oldest and least capable of Russian senior commanders. Marshal Semyon Budenny had been a highly talented cavalryman in his youth, rising from the ranks to achieve the rank of general. But in the 1920s he had been unimpressed by the early Russian tanks and had decided that they were useful only for siege warfare, and would be quite useless on the Russian steppes. He was one of only two marshals to survive Stalin's purges, owing his life to a slavish devotion to Stalin and his own brand of Communist ideology. When the war began, Budenny asked for orders from Moscow and thereafter did nothing without first having it approved by Stalin. The inevitable delays this caused, combined with his refusal to believe that tanks could move quickly across country, made Budenny a poor commander to face a 1941 blitzkrieg.

Rundstedt placed his Hungarian and Romanian allies (the Italians had not turned up on time) on the right wing, in the mountainous territory that suited their infantry better than his panzers. Their task was to begin a slow advance along the Black Sea coast towards Odessa, which would at the same time tie down much of the Red Army. The Germans, meanwhile, were concentrated in the north. He wanted to drive due east as far as Zhitomir, then turn south down the valley of the Bug River to surround all of the Red Army units facing the Romanians and the Hungarians. The Germans were then to move on to their next objective, the great naval port of Sevastopol on the Crimea. The capture of this port would render the Russian Black Sea Fleet as ineffective as Leeb was making the Baltic Fleet.

If this had not destroyed the Red Army ahead of

him, Rundstedt's next aim was to hook north to pin the remaining Russian units against Bock's forces. All being well, the Russian army in the south would then have been destroyed, the army's job would be over and it would be up to the politicians to arrange a peace deal.

This advance got off to a good start when the 6th Army, commanded by Walther von Reichenau, smashed through the Soviet 5th Army to reach Lutsk and Dubno in the first week. Once the Russian front line was breached, Rundstedt unleashed Ewald von Kleist and his 1st Panzer Group. The panzers headed east at speed, assisted by heavy *Luftwaffe* bombing raids. The 6th Army tried to keep up, but soon had their hands full rounding up prisoners.

Meanwhile, Rundstedt was concerned that the 25 Soviet divisions in the Carpathians might turn north to cut the supply lines feeding Kleist's panzer advance. He sent the 17th Army under General Carl-Heinrich von Stülpnagel to block this move, but was surprised to find that the Russians were retreating even before the German infantry arrived. Budenny was pulling his men back to defend the line of the Dniester River, even though Kleist's tanks were already east of that river and preparing to turn south down the Bug.

On 10 July, the 6th Army caught up with Kleist at Zhitomir and together the two forces turned south along the Bug. Unlike Timoshenko, Budenny failed to anticipate the Germans' moves and by 2 August his entire 6th and 12th Armies were encircled west of the Bug around Uman. Six days later 103,000 Soviets became prisoners.

Even before the Uman Pocket had been captured, Rundstedt was moving on to his next target, Sevastopol. He decided to leave the besieged Russian troops in Odessa to the Romanians.

German brutality

In these opening months, the brutal nature of the war became clear. Hitler had ordered that all Communist commissars – political officers attached to Red Army units – were to be shot dead. Behind the advancing German armies came large numbers of SS and Gestapo operatives and *Einsatzgruppen* ('Special Squads'), with orders to kill Jews and civic leaders without trial. The exact number of killings carried out by these teams is not clear because many records were later destroyed, but in 1941 alone more than 300,000 people – perhaps as many as 500,000 – were executed.

The extent to which the German army was aware of what was going on behind the lines is not clear. That the normal rule of law had been suspended in the occupied areas could not be hidden, nor could the fact that large numbers of people were being killed. However, many army officers claimed that they had been told that the *Einsatzgruppen* were merely concerned with combating the partisan and guerrilla groups who were attacking German supply lines.

Be that as it may, the frontline fighting was brutal from the start. Russia had never signed the Geneva Convention, which regulated how battles should be fought, how prisoners should be dealt with and how civilians were to be treated. Hitler had therefore felt justified in ordering the German army not to bother with the Convention in Russia, but to fight with the utmost ruthlessness. That they did so is shown by an account sent to Western newspapers by the Soviets in August 1941. It was a story dictated by Vasilav Dolgin, a Red Army machine-gunner, from his hospital bed.

'On 16 July we had orders to defend the village of Demidovo near Smolensk. I was wounded in the arm and leg. My commander told me to go back, but I wanted to give my ammunition to the other machine-gunner. I was trying to reach him when something crashed on my head and I fell unconscious.

'I lay where I was and regained consciousness only when I felt someone kicking me. I opened my eyes and saw a German officer and two soldiers. The officer ordered me to stand up, but I could not stand. The two soldiers pulled me to my feet, but when the officer hit me in the face with his fist I fell down again. Then the officer demanded to know the whereabouts of the Soviet troops

and how many tanks we had. I refused and he became angry and hit me again. I remained silent. He took a gun from one of the soldiers and shot me twice. The first bullet missed, but the second tore through my tongue and shattered several teeth. Thinking I was dead they left me.

'I was very weak and was bleeding badly. I wanted to dress my wounds, but I was afraid that if they saw the white bandage of my field dressing they would come back to kill me. I decided to remain as I was until the night and then try to reach the village and my comrades. The whole day I lay on the ground in a semi-conscious state. I had delusions of seeing my comrades and I wondered why they did not come to my rescue. I tried to call to them, but could not speak.

'Finally it was dark and I began to crawl to the village. I was seen by a Red Army man of the signal corps. He took me to a doctor who bandaged my wounds. Then I was put on a train to Moscow and here I am. That is all.'

Maintaining supplies

By the end of July, the Germans had won victories on a staggering scale. They had overrun vast areas of the western Soviet Union, smashed entire armies and captured close on a million prisoners. But they had not yet won the war. Hitler's plan to wipe out the Red Army in a series of mighty battles had failed, due to a combination of tenacious Russian resistance and poor roads for the German supply columns. A new dispute now broke out in the higher command echelons of the German army. The panzer commanders, such as Guderian, Kleist and Hoth, again began pushing their favoured strategy of deep, fast penetrations into the Soviet Union by large columns of armour, that would smash the Red Army and destroy its ability to organize itself. Others pointed out that the Germans were already as far, or further, into Russia than they had intended to go and that a further panzer advance would stretch supply lines to breaking point. They argued that the plan had miscarried only because of the unusually heavy July rains. Now that dry August weather could be expected, the original plan should be extended to engage the Red Army in a fresh round of battles of annihilation.

Again Hitler agreed with the more conventional approach. Inspecting the map for the best place to strike, he ordered Guderian to take his 2nd Panzer Group south to cut in behind the forces facing Rundstedt. The latter, meanwhile, was to ignore Sevastopol for the time being and instead strike north to meet Guderian and effect a massive encirclement of the Russian armies around Kiev.

Meanwhile, Hoth's panzers were likewise to be taken away from Bock's Army Group Centre. They were to go north to support Leeb in a renewed drive northeast to capture the great city of Leningrad.

The discussions took several days and more time slipped by while the necessary adjustments were made behind the lines. Supply routes and the disposition of fuel and ammunition dumps needed to be organized. It was at this point that the Germans first came across a problem that would become increasingly serious as the war progressed. Russian railway lines were not only few and far between, but they had been built by a variety of private companies to different plans over a number of decades. Often they did not connect with each other and, perhaps more crucially, they came in a variety of gauges. It was simply impossible to move rolling stock from one railway to another as needed by the army, nor was it possible to bring rolling stock from Germany. At this point in the war the German supply masters attacked the problem by recruiting large numbers of local men – often under appalling conditions – to manhandle crates and sacks from one wagon to another where different railways met.

By the spring of 1942, however, they had given up on this practice in favour of a more radical alternative. All Russian rolling stock was junked. Instead the Russian railways were converted from their strange mix of gauges to the standard German railway gauge. Locomotives and wagons were then brought from Germany to run on the newly converted railways. It was a lot of work to start with, but it saved huge amounts of effort later on.

Battle of Kiev

It was not until 21 August 1941 that the revised battle plan began to get under way. Guderian led the 2nd Panzer Group and the 2nd Army south from Smolensk and on 25 August seized the vital bridges over the Desna River near Konotop that could carry his tanks. He then swerved southeast to Romny. Meanwhile, Kleist had swung north from his drive to the Crimea and fought his way over the Dnieper River.

At the same time, the 6th and 17th Armies kept up the pressure as if launching a conventional infantry and artillery advance towards Kiev. This served to persuade Budenny to keep most of his surviving Southwest Front west of Kiev.

Sensing a possible disaster, Stalin sent Timoshenko to Kiev to have a look at things for himself. Once he arrived, Timoshenko held urgent talks with Budenny and with the head of the civilian government of Ukraine, Nikita Khrushchev. It seems that Khrushchev wanted to evacuate the city and most of Ukraine, pulling back to the Donetz River – but not before stripping the huge industrial city of its machinery and workers so that production could be set up elsewhere. Budenny, according to Khrushchev, was confident that he could fight a slow retreat that would give Khrushchev enough time to carry out his plan. But Timoshenko brought orders direct from Stalin. Kiev had to be held at all costs.

The city was not only a major centre of industry, agriculture and population – it was also a major cultural and religious centre that had been in existence since at least AD600, making it one of the oldest cities in the Soviet Union. There was also a political dimension. Ukraine had long been semi-autonomous within the Tsarist regime, but it had been strictly controlled by Moscow under the Communists. Stalin feared that, if Kiev fell, Ukraine might be set up by Hitler as an independent state and so start the unravelling of the Soviet Union. Hitler had no such plans, viewing the Ukrainians as every bit as backward as the Russians, but Stalin had good reason for his fears. Fifty years later the independence of Ukraine would indeed hasten the fall of the Soviet Union.

Timoshenko and Budenny began reorganizing the defence of Kiev, while Khrushchev told his men to stop dismantling machinery. It was to no avail. On 16 September Guderian and Kleist linked up near Lokhvitsa and Kiev was surrounded. Khrushchev decided to get out, slipping through the German lines while they were still thin, and he was soon followed by Timoshenko and Budenny. On 26 September around 620,000 Soviet soldiers surrendered, with another 300,000 or so having been killed in the fighting.

The drive for Moscow

In the north, Leeb had staged another great advance and had got Leningrad surrounded from the south, while the Finns encircled the north. Using his own panzers under Hoepner, and Hoth's from Army Group Centre, Leeb had punched through a defensive line the Russians were building on the Dnieper and had encircled almost a million men around Vyazma. The

Germans were not able to draw the noose tight at once and some 200,000 Soviets escaped. Nevertheless around 600,000 men were captured and 150,000 killed by the time the battle ended on 23 October.

Stalin then sacked Budenny and adopted a new pattern for organizing the high command of the Red Army. In future each army had its own permanent commander, but these generals were put under the control of marshals sent out from Moscow to organize and command specific operations. Stalin wanted to ensure that he always had the best man for the job in command of a particular area, while at the same time ensuring continuity of command at the army level.

It was now October and the autumn rains had come. And still the Russians were not beaten. It seemed that no matter how many men the Germans killed or captured, more appeared to take their place. The Germans had reckoned on the Russians being able to mobilize up to 200 divisions in the first six months of the war, but already they had fought and defeated 250 and another 100 were in the line against them.

Belatedly, Hitler decided to back those panzer generals who had argued in favour of a swift, narrow advance to capture key points. He gave orders for Hoepner and Guderian to drive for Moscow. But it was too late. The Russian winter weather was arriving and so too were fresh reinforcements from the Soviet far east. A Russian who was being evacuated east, along with his fellow factory workers and their equipment, was delayed when his train was shunted into a siding to make way for a troop train heading west. He recorded the following.

'I got the chance to walk across and visit the Red Army men in their carriages. The walls of every carriage were decorated with posters and newspapers, and with handwritten notes produced by the men themselves. Here was a call to smite the German hard "so that he'll never forget our plains and never think of coming to them again". There were caricatures of the enemy, drawn if not with skill then at least with wrath. One urged

---

railwaymen outright "We have been waiting and begging for this moment for four months, drive us faster comrades".

'I got into conversation with some of the men. They were artillerymen from Siberia, thickset, of no great height, but with seemingly inexhaustible strength. They apparently knew what they were in for, and they would probably fight like Siberians who are accustomed both to hard scraps and hard weather.'

On 2 December the Germans were in the suburbs of Moscow, but they never got any further. A Russian counterattack threw them back. The Soviet attack brought two new features to the battlefield that would come to dominate the Stalingrad campaign: the T34 tank and Marshal Georgy Zhukov.

3
WINTER PLANS

The Soviet counter-offensive in front of Moscow that was launched on 5 December 1941 had been made possible by one of the greatest espionage successes of the war. German Communist Richard Sorge had set up a spy network in Japan that from 1933 onwards had been providing Moscow with much valuable information about the Japanese government and industry. In late September 1941 Sorge was able to tell Moscow that Japan was not going to invade the mineral-rich areas of Soviet Siberia, but instead would strike south to secure the Dutch and British colonies, plus the Philippines.

The Soviet assault

Stalin was delighted by the news. It not only meant that he was not going to be fighting a war on two fronts, but it also allowed him to transfer large numbers of men from Siberia to protect Moscow. For some reason Stalin neglected to pass on the information to his British allies.

The Soviet assault not only drove the Germans back from Moscow, but it also made deep penetrations at various points along the front. In some places large numbers of German troops were cut off and surrounded. The move came as a huge shock to the German high command because they had thought that the Russians had no more troops in reserve. Instead of anticipating a swift victory come the spring, when the improved weather made panzer operations possible, the Germans now faced the prospect of a longer war. At once the disputes and debates about what to do began.

The Germans take stock

Looking back on the events so far, the Germans drew a number of lessons. The first of these was that Russia not only had vastly superior resources to Germany – most Germans had known that – but the Soviet system was also able to mobilize them much faster than had been anticipated. The Germans and their allies had begun the war with a slight superiority in terms of numbers. By December 1941 – and despite the vast losses sustained by the Soviets – the situation had reversed and now the Russians had a slight edge. The Russians were only going to mobilize more men, so the Germans now accepted that they would be outnumbered for the forseeable future.

This did not seem so bad in the light of the second lesson drawn by the Germans. The quality of German hardware was superior to that of the Soviets, but not markedly so. The new T34 tank showed that the Russians could produce weapons that were the equal of those used by the Germans, so the German generals began agitating for new, improved weaponry, especially tanks and anti-tank weapons. Rather more heartening was the fact that German tactics and training were clearly much better than those of the Russians. It had been the blitzkrieg tactic and the skill with which it was implemented that had won the Germans their great victories of 1941. Obviously, given time, the Russians would learn how to use similar tactics themselves, but for the foreseeable future the Germans had the edge.

The third lesson that many generals learned, though they did not dare say so, was that the bickering between Hitler and the OKW in August had cost them at least two, and possibly three, weeks of campaigning. Moscow could have been captured, and perhaps Leningrad as well, but the chance had been lost.

Disagreement and delay had been fatal, but this lesson could not be learned properly because the generals were still divided on how best to fight the Russians. Disagreements were bound to continue.

All things considered, the Germans still had a battlefield advantage over the Soviets, though the same could not be said for Germany's allies. The big question was how to use this advantage to bring the war to a successful conclusion.

Rundstedt and Leeb were both seriously worried

about the supply system. They were not only having trouble keeping their men supplied, but they were having to send increasing numbers of men back from the front line to guard supply lines against sabotage and pilfering by the local Russians. They believed that if 1942 were to see another move forward, deeper into Russia, the supply system would break down and expose the German troops to disaster. They both argued that it would be better to fall back to the western Soviet Union, where the roads were better and German factories were closer. Rundstedt even suggested going as far back as the Carpathians and the Nieman River, both of which formed natural and easily defended barriers. This meant returning almost to the start positions of June 1941. Although it made sound military sense, nobody took his idea seriously.

The majority of senior generals, however, did recognize that they were too far into Russia already. They opposed any massive new offensive and generally agreed that it would be best to fall back to a defensive position. Let the Red Army wear itself out assaulting their strong defences, they thought, then launch a blitzkrieg counterattack to surround and eliminate the exhausted survivors. The details of the different ideas varied, but all of them featured some variation or other on this basic plan.

Hitler, however, was not listening. Rundstedt lost patience with Hitler's views and fell out with him in spectacular fashion when Hitler vetoed Rundstedt's plan to fall back to a defensive line on the Mius River. Rundstedt resigned in November 1941. His place was taken by Field Marshal Walther von Reichenau of the 6th Army, but he died of a brain haemorrhage so Army Group South was then taken over by Bock, who until then had been commanding Army Group Centre. Reichenau's old command of the 6th Army was taken over by his deputy, Friedrich Paulus, who had drawn up the initial outline plans for a war with Russia back in 1940.

Army Group North also changed its commander. When the renewed drive on Leningrad failed to capture the city in December, Hitler had one of his increasingly frequent temper tantrums. He shouted his grievances at the OKW staff.

> 'Leeb is in a second childhood; he can't grasp and carry out my plan for the speedy capture of Leningrad. He fusses over his plan of assuming the defensive in the northwestern sector but wants a drive in the centre on Moscow. He's obviously senile. He has lost his nerve, and like a true Catholic he wants to pray but not fight.'

When Leeb heard of this tirade in January 1942 he resigned, claiming ill-health. He was replaced by Georg von Küchler, who had a long history of anti-Communist activity but was not as talented a military commander as Leeb. It was a sign that Hitler was beginning to favour political reliability over military competence in his choice of generals.

Perhaps the most important change in the German high command came on 10 December when Walther von Brauchitsch resigned as Commander-in-Chief of the German army. Brauchitsch was one of the most talented staff officers of his generation. His work on deciding which roads different units should take, how they should advance and how they should be supplied had been instrumental in the successes in Poland in 1939 and France in 1940, as well as the initial stages of the invasion of Russia. More importantly, he was one of the very few senior generals who felt able to stand up to Hitler. His mixture of flattery, conciliation and contradiction had more than once induced Hitler to alter plans and objectives. By late 1941 this ability was waning and it might have been the stress of repeated, hot-tempered confrontations with Hitler that caused the heart attack that now forced his resignation.

Hitler did not replace Brauchitsch. Instead he appointed himself Commander-in-Chief of the army. In the short run this gave Hitler greater control over the conduct of the war and made the army more compliant to his will. In the long term it proved to be a poor move, because Hitler was unable to devote the time to the task that it deserved and he refused to delegate to others. Decisions went unmade, policies were undecided and delays multiplied. In December 1941 all of that lay in the future. What was important at the time was that it ensured that only Hitler would decide what was going to happen in 1942.

Hitler not only had reports from the army on his desk but also reports from the heads of the civilian departments in Germany, plus those of the occupying forces in the conquered countries. All painted a fairly bleak picture, with each report demanding additional men, *matériel* and cash. In part, these demands were traditional bureaucratic demands for a larger slice of the cake, but they also reflected the fact that Germany was overstretched. The OKW estimated that it needed another 800,000 men to launch a large-scale, general offensive in Russia in 1942, but Albert Speer, who was in charge of German industry, reported that if he released that number of men from the factories there would be no weapons or munitions with which the army could fight.

The key report, however, proved to be one about

Germany's energy demands. This stated that the increased war effort was consuming vastly greater quantities of coal and oil than had been anticipated. It predicted that if something was not done fairly quickly, the German armaments industries would run out of coal and the German army would run out of oil. Hitler knew that there was plenty of coal in Ukraine, some of it already under German control, and that there was even more oil in the Caucasus. He therefore decided that the main thrust for the German campaign in 1942 would be in the south.

In deciding to capture the rest of Ukraine and the Caucasus oilfields, Hitler was also preparing the way for what he hoped to achieve in 1943. Assuming all went well in 1942, the German armies would end up on the shores of the Caspian Sea at Astrakhan. From there it would be possible in 1943 to thrust north up the valley of the mighty Volga. The Germans could then sweep west to take Moscow from the rear, surrounding and annihilating the vast Russian armies in the area. Alternatively they could divert east to take and destroy the remaining armaments factories that were turning out Soviet tanks and guns. Hitler seems to have considered both possibilities at various times, but he put off a decision until the Caucasus campaign was over.

A smaller effort would be made in the north, to capture Leningrad and link up with the Finns. No major campaign was planned for the centre due to a lack of resources. There would, however, be minor offensives, designed to open up reliable supply lines to the isolated German forward positions.

The Russian winter

Of rather more immediate concern than all of these plans for the 1942 campaign was the problem of what to do over the winter of 1941. Because they had been expecting the war to be over by the autumn, the Germans had not manufactured enough winter clothing for all of their men but only for the smaller number that had been expected to stay in Russia as an army of occupation. In Hungary, Admiral Horthy knew exactly what to do. He ordered all of his men to come home, promising the outraged Hitler that the Hungarians would return in the spring. The Germans had no such choice.

Instead Hitler ordered that the German army was to stand and fight where it stood. In the wake of the Soviet offensive of December, that meant holding a highly convoluted line with some isolated pockets. The Germans came to refer to this situation as a 'hedgehog', with each forward-thrusting peninsula of German-held territory likened to a hedgehog's spike with a sharp and dangerous tip. The way in which the Soviet advance had developed meant that the Russians had advanced quickest and farthest in open country, but had made barely any headway against towns that had been fortified, or strongly held, by the Germans. Each forward prong of German-held land was tipped by a town such as Vyazma, Orel, Kursk, Kharkov or Briansk. In many cases the hedgehog spines contained a road along which supplies could be moved up, but in some instances the outlying German-held town had no such link.

This was where the *Luftwaffe* came in. Transport aircraft were brought up and bombers hurriedly converted, so that food and ammunition could be flown in to the beleaguered garrisons and the injured flown out. Goering, the head of the *Luftwaffe*, surpassed himself in the winter of 1941 by overcoming enormous technical and logistical problems to keep the supply aircraft flying. He was helped greatly by the fact that the Soviet air force had been almost annihilated in the first months of war and was only just starting to rebuild itself. It was the *Luftwaffe* and its supply flights that allowed the isolated army posts to hold on.

However, the hard wear and tear of long and frequent flights in bitter winter weather exerted a strain on pilots and aircraft that exhausted both men and machines. During the spring of 1942 the *Luftwaffe* would be more concerned with rebuilding itself than with fighting the Soviets in the air. The Russians were allowed to regain a measure of air power on which they would later build, gaining air superiority by 1944. The process was only just starting in 1942, but already the German soldiers on the ground noticed the increased presence of enemy aircraft.

On the ground the German, Italian and Romanian soldiers suffered terribly. The Russian winter is notoriously cold, snowy and windy. By and large the majority of troops did not have good enough clothing to withstand the temperatures for long. Frostbite became relatively common, along with lethargy and exhaustion. There were also major problems with equipment. The oil used to lubricate panzer engines would freeze solid unless the engines were run for a few minutes every couple of hours. The Italian infantry found that the gap between a trigger and its guard was too small for a gloved finger to be inserted, so they could not shoot without taking off their gloves and risking frostbite. Casualties were not unduly high, but discomfort was, and many units found that fewer and fewer men were fit for duty as the winter passed.

All of these problems meant that the German army would not be ready to launch its offensives until late in May 1942. The campaign of 1940 had begun on 9 April in Norway, that of 1941 on 6 April in Yugoslavia. The later start date was a sign of increasing strain on the German military system.

Operation Blue

The plan for the southern offensive, as it finally emerged from the OKW, under Hitler's personal influence, was codenamed Operation Blue. It consisted of a number of preliminary moves designed to mask and conceal the single main thrust to the southeast. The first move was to be in the Crimea, where two pockets of Soviet troops still held out. The great naval port of Sevastopol lay in the southeast of the Crimea, its Russian garrison greatly boosted by men evacuated from Odessa by the Soviet navy. The city was surrounded by massive fortifications equipped with numerous heavy guns. The siege had already begun, but it was to be stepped up with the aim of capturing the city by midsummer. In the east of the Crimea the Russians were still holding on to the Kerch Peninsula. The attack here was to be launched on 8 May, with one week allowed for the peninsula to be captured. The capture of the peninsula was important, not only because it drove the Soviets out of the Crimea but also because it was only a short hop across the Kerch Strait to the mainland far behind the Soviet lines.

For the main part of the offensive, Hitler had greatly reinforced Army Group South and then divided it into two new formations: Army Group A and Army Group B. The southern part of the front was given to Army Group A. This consisted of the 11th Army, the 17th Army and the 1st Panzer Army (formerly the 1st Panzer Group) plus the 4th Romanian Army. Command was given to Wilhelm von List, who had served in Poland, France and Greece. List was given the task of completing the strategic goal of the campaign by capturing the Caucasus oilfields.

The northern part of the offensive was the responsibility of Army Group B, under the command of Maximilian von Weichs, formerly commander of the 2nd Army in Army Group Centre. Weichs was given the 2nd Army, the 6th Army, the 4th Panzer Army, the Italian 8th Army and the Hungarian 2nd Army. Their task was twofold – to launch misleading opening attacks and then to act as a northern flank guard for Army Group A, to stop Russian attacks coming down from the north and interfering with the drive to the oilfields.

Army Group B was to move first, driving due east from the line between Kursk and Kharkov to reach the Don River opposite Voronezh. Such an advance could easily be aimed at breaching the Don before swinging north to attack Moscow from the south. It was hoped that the Soviets would assume that this was the German plan, especially as small assaults would be launched in front of Moscow at the same time. If the Soviets moved their reserves to protect the southern flank of Moscow, they would make the real German target easier to achieve.

Having reached the Don, Army Group B was then

to swing south down the river bank. The German units were to lead the way, clearing the Soviets from the west bank and leaving behind allied units to guard the river against a counterattack. Only when Army Group B reached the great bend in the Don below Voroshilovgrad would it cross the river and drive east. At this point there was a narrow neck of land between the Don and the even larger Volga. Weichs was then to continue down the Volga to the Caspian. The Don–Volga line was to be held by Army Group B, cutting off the Caucasus from the rest of the Soviet Union.

The city of Stalingrad stood on the west bank of the Volga beside the narrow neck of land between the two rivers.

Its capture was considered desirable, but not essential. A good defensive line drawn south of the city would do.

Meanwhile, Army Group A was to launch its offensive in mid-July, once Army Group B was moving down the Don. It was to advance to Rostov, cross the River Don and then drive fast across the vast Kalmyk

Steppe to reach the Caspian and the oilfields. Hitler hoped that most Soviet reserves would have been drawn north to protect Moscow and that List would have little trouble reaching the distant oilfields.

The Soviet advance

The Soviets had also been looking back over 1941, drawing lessons and planning their moves for 1942. A Moscow newspaper summed up what many in the Russian capital felt in December 1941.

'The Nazi invaders are being beaten now not by the frost, but by our glorious Red Army. And the frosts – the real Russian frosts – are still ahead. The Nazi hordes are rolling back. The roads are strewn with the bodies of German soldiers, burnt and damaged vehicles and guns. Such is the inglorious end of the second great offensive against Moscow, proclaimed by Hitler. The promised peace has not materialized for the German people. The promised rest in warm houses in Moscow has not materialized for the

German troops. The rout of Hitler's elite divisions
with colossal fresh losses has resulted in a complete
failure of his plans to capture Moscow.'

Emboldened by the success of their December offensive at Moscow, the Soviets were inclined to launch further offensives in 1942. In the south, they planned to begin with an offensive in the Crimea. While the Germans intended to drive the Russians out of the Kerch Peninsula, the Russians were going to use the same peninsula as a springboard for a drive to push the Germans out of the Crimea.

Further north, the Soviets planned an offensive across the Volkhov River towards Luga. The aim was to get behind the German forces besieging Leningrad from the south and force them to retreat. The offensive was the task of the Volkhov Front.

The main Soviet effort for the summer was, however, to take the form of a twin offensive, with one branch heading toward Kholm and the other aimed at Kharkov. The Kholm Offensive was to be launched by three fronts – the Northwest Front, the Kalinin Front and the West Front – driving west between Lake Ilmen in the north and Rzhev in the south. This assault was designed to be a conventional attack conducted by infantry, accompanied by a few tanks and preceded by an artillery barrage. It would have been a plan familiar to men in the trenches of 1916. The Kharkov Offensive, however, was to be the first Russian attempt at copying German blitzkrieg tactics and was to include the bulk of the Russian tank units.

This twin offensive was rather optimistically designed to inflict a crushing blow on the German Army Group Centre and begin the liberation of western Russia. The Russians even briefed British diplomats in Moscow on the projected success of the attack. The diplomat cabled back to London that

'This offensive will throw the Nazis back a long way. A new German offensive is anticipated in the spring, which may make some limited headway into Russia but it will not achieve much. Then the

Russians intend to give the coup de grace in the autumn or winter. I do not think the Russians will stop at the German borders, but are out to defeat Germany conclusively and for ever.'

At the time, the message was treated sceptically in London. The German army appeared to be so superior to the Red Army that such predictions by the Soviets were dismissed as mere bombastic wishful thinking. Events were to prove that this message from January 1942 was not so ridiculous after all.

It was the Soviets who struck first, on 7 January, on the Volkhov. The offensive was spearheaded by the 2nd Shock Army, backed up by the Volkhov Front. The Volkhov Front was commanded by Marshal Kirill Meretskov, with General Andrei Vlasov as his deputy. The two men were very different. Meretskov was an old-style commander who had been arrested during Stalin's purge of the army and had only narrowly escaped execution. Vlasov was a talented younger officer tipped to rise to the very top. Vlasov led the

2nd Shock Army in person, carefully organizing the men and training them in new tactics.

The offensive began well. With the advantage of the winter weather, Vlasov managed to punch a 20-kilometre-wide (12.4-mile) hole in the German lines and over the days that followed he advanced steadily to finally reach a point 72 kilometres (45 miles) from his start lines. Meretskov, however, pushed forward the promised supporting units only slowly and with orders not to go too far. The advance stuttered to a halt. When the spring weather came the Germans counterattacked near the base of the Russian advance, cutting off Vlasov and the 2nd Shock Army. Stalin sent a light plane to rescue Vlasov, but he refused and stayed with his men. In all 35,000 men of the 2nd Shock Army were captured, 30,000 were killed and barely 8,000 escaped. Vlasov later tried to persuade the Germans to allow him to raise an army of anti-Communists from among the huge numbers of Russian prisoners, but the offer was turned down.

Two days after the abortive Volkhov Offensive had begun, the much larger Kholm Offensive started, under the command of Pavel Kurochkin. From the Soviet point of view, the attack was a great success. The German front line collapsed, allowing the Russians to surge forward in massed formations.

The Demyansk Pocket

The town of Demyansk was surrounded by the Soviet tide, trapping the German 12th, 30th, 32nd, 123rd and 290th infantry divisions, plus the SS-Division *Totenkopf*. Under the command of General Walter Graf von Brockdorff-Ahlefeldt, the Germans dug in, built a temporary airfield to ensure a chain of supplies and awaited the inevitable onslaught.

Meanwhile the Russian advance rolled on across a broad frontage to reach some 120 kilometres (75 miles) from the start lines, with some units getting almost 160 kilometres (100 miles) from where they had started. Lieutenant-General Konstantin Golubev captured the town of Yaroslavets (Maloyaroslavets) on the first day of the attack. His report ran:

'We found tanks, armoured cars and guns in good order literally at every step. Large fuel and ammunition dumps were intact. We captured about 50 enemy tanks and armoured cars, about 100 lorries, over 60 guns, over 150 machine-guns, 500 bicycles and whole depots of shells, explosives, cartridges, grenades and fuel. The enemy is fleeing and losing his elite cadres of men and officers.'

Kurochkin was jubilant. The captured stores were handed out to the Russian units and turned against the Germans. But he was not to know that his success was largely down to a lack of German defenders and reserves. When these began arriving by train in large numbers the Soviet advance ground to a halt. It had been particularly deficient in tanks and once German forces came up the lack of Soviet armour began to show.

However, the Germans on the central front lacked the means for a large counterattack, so the units at Demyansk remained cut off. They were kept supplied by the *Luftwaffe*, which flew in thousands of tons of supplies, airlifted out the wounded and even brought in reinforcements when needed. What followed was to be an epic of military endurance that was quoted extensively by the German propaganda ministry under Josef Goebbels. For political reasons much emphasis was put on the exploits of the SS men at Demyansk, but the ordinary German soldier was given a lot of credit as well.

Large amounts of newspaper articles and newsreel footage were produced to push the key points that the Nazis wanted the world to know about Demyansk. Wounded men airlifted out of the pocket were patched up, given smart new uniforms and made available to newspapermen from neutral nations for interview. Profile pieces on the men at Demyansk and their loving families at home were featured in German newspapers and magazines. According to Goebbels the story of Demyansk was that a heroic handful of Aryan warriors was holding out against the odds and inflicting massive damage on the barbarians who sought to spread the evils of Communism across Europe. It was inspiring stuff that made a big impression on the German public and on Hitler, who appreciated the value of propaganda in warfare.

Meanwhile a great military parade was held in Moscow to mark the 24th anniversary of the day the Red Army first went into battle – 23rd February 1918. Stalin made a long speech that concluded:

'The Red Army's strength rests above all in the fact that it does not wage a predatory imperialistic war, but a patriotic war, a war of liberation, a just war. The Red Army's task is to liberate our Soviet territory from the German invaders, the residents of our towns and villages who, before the war, were free and lived like human beings and who are now oppressed and suffer pillage, subjection and famine – and lastly to liberate our women from the outrages to which they have been subjected by the Fascist fiends.

'The Red Army has to annihilate the German Fascist occupationists since they wish to enslave our Motherland, or when they are being surrounded

refuse to lay down their arms and surrender. The Red Army annihilates them because they seek to enslave our Motherland. The Red Army, like any army of any other people, is entitled to annihilate and bound to annihilate the enslavers of our Motherland.'

The Nazi propaganda chief, Goebbels, made sure that the defenders in Demyansk got to read the final paragraph, to show them that they could expect little mercy from the Soviet soldiers. It was not quite what Stalin had in mind. Finally, in April, a German counterattack launched from the northern flank of the Russian bulge broke through to Demyansk and the trapped men were withdrawn.

On 27 February the Soviet offensive in the Crimea opened on the Kerch Peninsula. The local German commander, Erich von Manstein of the 11th Army, had prepared his defences well and the Russian assault failed, amidst terrible casualties. The Russians tried again on 15 March and then a third time on 16 March, but each time their efforts collapsed and they took heavy casualties.

Meanwhile, all eyes were turning to Ukraine where both the Russians and the Germans had major operations planned.

4
CASE BLUE

The Soviet offensive to capture Kharkov, the third-largest city in the Soviet Union, and then drive on west was a carefully devised plan based on an imperfect understanding of how blitzkrieg worked. That misunderstanding would prove disastrous for the Soviets.

Second Battle of Kharkov

The Russians had correctly noted that an initial breakthrough was usually achieved by a combined force of tanks, infantry and artillery. Thereafter, tanks and infantry riding in lorries raced ahead as a combined unit, usually with air support, to penetrate deeply behind enemy lines, spreading confusion and seizing key points. Meanwhile the conventional infantry marched up behind to secure supply lines and overwhelm any remaining opposition. They had also correctly observed that the more successful German operations in 1941 had involved two pincer columns, spearheaded by panzers, that had pushed deep into enemy territory before swinging inwards to close shut and surround the hapless defenders.

What the Russian planners had missed were the close radio communications that had been established and maintained between the various army units and the *Luftwaffe*, and the need to keep the racing panzers supplied with fuel and ammunition wherever they went. The Soviet supply system was simply not flexible enough to cope with a rapidly changing advance, nor was the Soviets' communications network able to keep the different units in touch. The result was that while the Red Army could follow a pre-arranged plan well enough, it could not change its dispositions or supply routes quickly enough to cope with a changing situation. And the essence of blitzkrieg was the ability to adapt and take advantage of opportunities as they arose.

Stalin put Timoshenko in charge of the operation to recapture Kharkov and gave him considerable forces. In all, the Southwest Front was given 640,000 men, 1,200 tanks and 950 aircraft for the operation. Not only did Timoshenko have more tanks than the Germans facing him, but he also had nearly all of the T34 and KV1 tanks that were battle ready. The T34 medium tank was the equal of the German Panzer IV, while the KV1 was a virtually invulnerable, heavily-armoured tank, whose only drawback was its slow speed.

Timoshenko organized this vast force into two pincers. The northern pincer would drive east from

Volchansk and reach west of Kharkov before turning south. It comprised the 28th and 57th Armies, with around 400 tanks. The southern pincer consisted of the 6th and 9th Armies, with 800 tanks. It was based at Izyum and was to head east to Krasnograd. Once there the Soviet 6th Army was to swing north to link up with the northern pincer, in order to trap the Germans in Kharkov. The 9th Army, meanwhile, was to turn south towards the Black Sea, to ensnare the German units in the area.

The attack was launched on 12 May with Timoshenko issuing an Order of the Day that was read out to each unit involved.

'I hereby order the troops to begin the decisive offensive against our vilest enemy, the German Fascist Army, to exterminate its men and exterminate its war materials, and to hoist our glorious Soviet banner over the liberated cities and villages of Russia.'

And the offensive began well. In the north the Russian 28th and 57th Armies struck the German 6th Army commanded by Paulus. Without any natural barriers to help him, Paulus opted for a fighting retreat. He kept his line intact, but fell back slowly before the onslaught. In the south the main Soviet tank strength had struck some Romanian units, which soon gave way. The Soviets burst through in large numbers, opening up a gap 48 kilometres (30 miles) wide in the German lines. Again Paulus opted for a fighting retreat while Kleist, to the south, moved his units up to stop the Russians widening the gap or swinging south.

A Soviet newspaper reporter, who was with the leading troops of the southern pincer, sent back a report to his editor.

'Spring has set in and our armies are rolling ahead across fields already covered with young grass. The rumble of tanks fills the air and above, heading westward, drone the fleets of our bombers. Men with flags stand at our bridges, at river crossings,

directing the vehicles towards the front. At one point soldiers have found time to write out in mighty letters of stone, placed across the hillside, the words "Forward to the West". Back through the recaptured villages are pouring columns of German prisoners, men with glassy faces who do not yet understand what has happened. Many of them are youngsters of 18. These are Hitler's reserves.'

The commander of Army Group South, Bock, very quickly realized that the Russian assault was being spearheaded by a mass of their most modern tanks, but he guessed that support would be lacking. In this he was correct. Most of the supplies for the Russian tank units were being transported on horse-drawn carts. These simply could not keep up with the tanks. Moreover the few supply lorries were not accompanied by truck-mounted anti-aircraft guns and were therefore vulnerable to air attack. Bock wanted to lure the Soviet armour on, then counterattack at the base of the new bulge, to cut off the main Russian units and surround them.

Bock telephoned Franz Halder, the head of the Army General Staff (*Oberkommando des Heeres* or OKH) to seek permission for his plan. Halder took the plan to Hitler, feeling that it was such a large operation that it needed the Führer's personal permission. Hitler looked at the maps, read the reports and then pounced on Bock's idea. He rapidly sketched out which units should be used and thereafter claimed the idea as his own. Halder sent Hitler's permission to Bock, followed by a stream of increasingly detailed instructions on how the operation should be conducted. These were then passed on to Paulus and Kleist, who for the first time were exposed to Hitler's interference in detail.

While Paulus and Kleist were moving their units up as directed by Hitler, the Russians were continuing to advance. The northern pincer was making only slow progress, but in the south the main armoured thrust was roaring ahead. On 17 May the two armies diverged, as planned. The 9th Army found itself in open country with not a German in sight. The tanks drove on as if on a leisure tour and by dusk they were 112 kilometres (70 miles) from their start lines.

Back at Timoshenko's headquarters, however, the first hints of trouble were heard. A report came in from a unit on the southern flank of the southern advance, that spoke of the sighting of large numbers of German tanks. By now Timoshenko was growing concerned about adequate supplies reaching his leading tank units, and this new threat made him reach for the telephone. At midnight he got through to the Stavka, the Russian army headquarters, and spoke to Georgy Malenkov, Stalin's right-hand man on the all-powerful State Defence Committee. Timoshenko outlined the position, then asked if he could halt his advance until he had secured the flanks of the bulge against what looked like being serious counteroffensives. Malenkov refused and curtly told Timoshenko to get on with capturing Kharkov.

Next morning Kleist burst through the thinly-held southern flank of the Russian bulge. By dusk the Russian forces were in confusion. Timoshenko again telephoned the Stavka, this time saying he had to retreat. Again he was told to stop being defeatist and to push on to Kharkov. Next day Paulus attacked southwards and by 23 May the main Soviet forces in the southern pincer were surrounded. The Russian 6th and 57th Armies were trapped, apart from a few units. A week of savage fighting followed, and at its end the two Soviet armies were annihilated. The Germans took 240,000 prisoners, left some 50,000 Russian dead in the fields and destroyed or captured 950 tanks and 200 guns. They had lost only 20,000 dead or wounded.

The battles also cost the lives of thousands of horses, on which the Soviet army relied for the transport of supplies in the combat area. An official from the British Royal Society for the Prevention of Cruelty to Animals visited a frontline veterinary hospital as part of a fact-finding mission for a fund-raising drive in Britain, which aimed to provide equipment to help Russian horses. When he returned to Britain he wrote:

'I spoke with the official responsible for establishing veterinary services in the areas recovered from the

Germans as the Red Army advanced. I learned that about 60% of cases of injury to horses are to the legs, either from cuts on obstacles or inflammation of joints. When I asked if such cases of lameness were treated locally in the combat area I was told this was impossible and that such horses were sent to the rear for treatment. I carried away from my visit an impression that the men were fully aware of the value of the work that the horses were doing.'

The battles around Kharkov had produced two results that would prove crucial to the Stalingrad campaign. First, Timoshenko had lost 80 per cent of his tanks and most of his artillery, as well as a large proportion of his men. It would take time to make up these losses and with the main German offensive about to open Timoshenko did not have that time.

The second result was that Friedrich Paulus, commander of the German 6th Army, was lauded in the German press as a new hero. The decision by propaganda chief Goebbels to give Paulus the star treatment was largely political. Goebbels wanted to boost civilian morale at home after the failure to beat Russia in 1941, and thought Paulus ideal. He had been born the son of a poor schoolteacher and had dropped out of university due to a lack of funds. He had then joined the army and had worked his way up through the ranks by sheer hard work and dedication, earning a creditable record in action in the trenches of the First World War along the way. He could therefore be presented as an ideal of triumph over adversity and as a genuine working-class hero – as well as a shining example of what Aryan soldiers could achieve against the subhuman Russians. By contrast, the other commander involved, Kleist, was an aristocrat who had enjoyed all the advantages of wealth and privilege.

German summer offensive

With the Russian offensives destroyed, Bock could concentrate on his own plans. He did a quick survey of his forces and decided that the losses and disruption he had suffered had been only minor. The main offensive would open as planned on 28 June.

First of all the Kerch Peninsula had been cleared. There had been three Soviet armies on the peninsula – the 44th, the 47th and the 51st under Dimitri Kozlov, who had constructed strong defensive lines after the failure of his assaults earlier in the year. His opponent, Manstein, had begun the operation in April, with bombing raids which had seriously reduced the flow of supplies to the Russians across the Kerch Strait.

On 8 May the *Luftwaffe* had switched to bombing Soviet command communication positions, most of which had been destroyed by dusk. At dawn next day the ground offensive had begun with panzers punching through holes in the defences, cleared for them by Stuka dive bombers.

Already short on food and ammunition, and now bereft of orders, the Soviet forces had fled. Kozlov had then ordered the peninsula to be evacuated by sea and had managed to get away with 110,000 men before the panzers had captured the port at Kerch on 20 May. The Soviets had lost 130,000 men killed or captured. Manstein had lost only 600 men dead and 2,600 wounded. It was an auspicious opening move in the great summer offensive.

A second preliminary move was made on 10 June when the Germans crossed the Donets River at Izyum, then turned north to Belgorod, securing a slice of territory on the east bank of the river. Into this area moved not only the 6th Army under Paulus, but also the 1st Panzer Army under Kleist. To the north of the 6th Army, near Kursk, the 4th Panzer Army and the 2nd Army formed up. Writing from Moscow a British reporter concluded:

'Von Bock's renewal of the attack in the Kharkov area was evidently a preliminary operation. It met with little success and was immensely costly. If and when a major offensive does come, these preliminary operations may have robbed it of much of its sting. Moscow Radio has commented on the failure of panzers against the new power

of anti-tank guns and draws the conclusion that deep penetration by panzer thrusts are unlikely to be attempted in future. That, of course, will mean slower operations than those of last year.'

As events would show, this was either wishful thinking or mere propaganda on the part of the Soviets.

The Stavka (Soviet military high command) had taken note of the large numbers of panzers that had destroyed their offensive at Kharkov. They concluded that the main German offensive would take place in this area and speculated that it would strike east to cross the Don at Voronezh before either turning north to Moscow or south to the Caucasus oilfields. Voronezh was linked to Moscow by a railway line down which supplies and reinforcements could be rushed, so Timoshenko was ordered to hold the city at all costs.

The first German units to move were the 2nd Army and the 4th Panzer Army, which struck east from Kursk. The Soviet 40th Army collapsed almost at once when Hoth's panzers tore a gap in the front line, and then drove on to disrupt and destroy the command centres and supply lines. Two other armies, the 21st and the 28th, were driven back, but managed to stay reasonably intact. The 13th Army in the north suffered least and drew back farther north. The German 2nd Army then made a short but strong thrust north as if heading towards Moscow. The move alarmed Stalin, who summoned all the Soviet reserves to concentrate around the Soviet capital. The move was, of course, a feint designed to achieve exactly this result.

Two days after the first attack, the 6th Army and the 1st Panzer Army also moved. Again they drove due east, towards Cherkovo. Again Soviet resistance in front of them collapsed, allowing the Germans to move forward with barely a check. The landscape was on the side of the Germans, for the area was made up of huge, open plains covered by grassland or grain fields. There were no swamps or forests to impede the progress of the panzers and despite what Moscow Radio had to say the Red Army could not stop them either.

Within a week the Germans were on the Don and

had crossed the river to take Voronezh. Timoshenko had orders to hold this city, so he launched a counteroffensive that regained Voronezh from the Germans, for whom it was merely a secondary target. The 2nd Panzer Army then turned southeast along the Don, clearing out Soviet resistance, and the 2nd Army marched up behind to smash any opposition that remained. The Hungarians, meanwhile, toiled up behind the 6th Army to dig in along the Don in defensive positions, to guard the flank and rear of the Germans. At the same time, the 1st Panzer Army had reached Cherkovo and turned south towards Rostov and the lower Don, while the 6th Army marched on east to join the 4th Panzer Army. At this point the 17th Army moved forward along the Black Sea coast to march on Rostov, aiming to reach that city at the same time as the 1st Panzer Army.

The sacking of Bock

Timoshenko's counterattack at Voronezh was to have a profound if unintended effect on the campaign.

Bock, commander of Army Group South, was impressed by the strength of the counterattack. As commander of Army Group Centre in 1941, he had seen time and again how a powerful Soviet presence on a flank had forced a slowdown in the German advance and had at times threatened to upset the German offensive entirely. Bock therefore wanted to deal with the strong Soviet forces around Voronezh, under the command of Nikolai Vatutin.

On 12 July Bock suggested to Halder at the OKH that the 2nd Army and part of Hoth's 4th Panzer Army should be sent back north over the Don to crush this threat to his flank. The 6th Army would meanwhile continue down the Don River while the rest of the 4th Panzer Army would race ahead to the Volga, seizing the neck of land between the two rivers and the city of Stalingrad. Given that the Soviet resistance along the Don was now non-existent, the plan had merit.

Bock's request sent Hitler into a furious rage. Bock was without doubt one of Germany's most talented senior commanders, but he had already infuriated

Hitler twice. The first dispute had come in August 1941 when Hitler had ordered Guderian's panzers south to aid Rundstedt at Kiev. Bock had argued passionately and at length that Rundstedt should fight his own battles and that Guderian should drive down the open road to Moscow. At that stage in the war, Hitler was still open to alternative proposals put forward by his generals but was becoming intolerant of those who disagreed with him once he had made his mind up. Bock continued arguing long after it would have been wise for him to have accepted Hitler's decision.

The second dispute seems to have been more serious so far as Hitler was concerned, though it was outwardly less dramatic and certainly more short-lived. During the winter of 1941 Bock had sent a formal written protest to the OKW about the way in which the SS, the Gestapo and other non-army units were treating the civilian population in conquered areas of the Soviet Union. This treatment was excessively brutal with mass executions of Jews being widespread, rape and murder common and the use of slave labour under appalling conditions not at all unusual. Unlike many army officers further down the chain of command, Bock got to hear about the outrages. He viewed these physical manifestations of Nazi racial ideology to be not only morally wrong but also militarily counter-productive, because they would stir up resistance. Hitler, of course, fully supported the murders, killings and mistreatment of the subhuman Russians and was infuriated by Bock's protest.

Bock's request to return to Voronezh came at a particularly bad time, because Hitler was jubilantly enjoying the reports of collapsing Soviet resistance all along the southern front. Vast new conquests were being made and massive advances were being achieved. A furious Hitler sacked Bock on the spot. Henceforth List, the commander of Army Group A, and Weichs, commanding Army Group B, were to be entirely independent, with no Army Group South overall commander co-ordinating their actions.

The growing importance of Stalingrad

Four days after Bock was sacked, the Soviet Stavka issued orders to the authorities in Stalingrad. They were told to prepare to defend their city. It was the first sign the Stavka had given that they considered a thrust to Stalingrad a real possibility. As the local authorities began to evacuate women and children, barricade streets and stockpile food, orders were sent out to move reserves to the city.

General Vasily Chuikov was in the process of licking the 64th Army into shape at Tula when he received orders to go to Stalingrad and be in defensive positions by 19 July. Chuikov at once saw that the orders were impossible. Not only were his men mostly reservists who had barely got used to wearing uniforms, never mind become proficient in tactical manoeuvres, but they had to march 200 kilometres (125 miles) on foot in just two days. He rather bravely objected to the orders and was told that he could be in position by 21 July instead. In fact it was 23 July before he got there. Other troops were also appearing. When he arrived Chuikov found the Soviet 21st Army taking up position just north of Stalingrad. The Soviet defence was still sketchy and would have been unable to stand up to a single German army, but it was getting stronger by the day.

With Bock out of the way, Hitler began intervening even more than usual in the conduct of the campaign. On 23 July new orders were sent to List and Weichs. List had reported coming up against increasing resistance in the broken country in front of Rostov. Hitler had also noticed that his armies were failing to make the great captures of prisoners that had been the rule in 1941. This was partly due to the fact that there were fewer Soviet soldiers in the area and partly the result of Timoshenko pulling back rather than standing still to be surrounded. Now Hitler sensed a chance to inflict serious losses. He ordered Hoth's 4th Panzer Army to swing south to attack Rostov from the east and surround the Soviets facing Kleist's 1st Panzer Army and the 17th Army. The 6th Army would continue east on foot to capture Stalingrad.

The order was crucial for two reasons. First, it diverted Hoth away from his primary objective of securing the Don–Volga line. Originally, it was to have been the fast-moving, hard-hitting panzers that were to capture and establish this defensive flank line, while the infantry were to take over once the positions had been won. Second, it was the first time that the actual capture of Stalingrad had been made a key objective. Previously, the most important objective had been securing the south bank of the Volga, with Stalingrad to be taken only if possible.

If the reason for the first change – Hitler's desire for a victory at Rostov – can be easily understood, the reasons for the second are not so straightforward. With hindsight the decision to attack and capture Stalingrad turned out to be a huge mistake, so those German generals who survived the war were keen to avoid responsibility and quick to pin the blame on Hitler. Some suggested that Hitler believed that the line of the lower Volga could not be held against Soviet counterattacks unless Stalingrad was secured first. Others theorized that it was the name of the city that attracted Hitler. The city had been named Tsaritsyn when it had been founded in 1589, but after the fall of Tsarist rule it had been renamed to honour Stalin, just as St Petersburg had been renamed to honour Lenin. Another school of thought had it that Hitler wanted to launch an offensive up the Volga valley in 1943 and viewed the capture of Stalingrad as a necessary pre-emptive move.

There is always a temptation to explain great events in terms of great ambitions, but the truth about Stalingrad might be much simpler. In the orders of 23 July Stalingrad was only one among many other targets and aims. It had no obvious priority over the others. It might be that the first failure to capture the city led to reinforcements being sent to make a second attempt, which also failed. More reserves were then fed in to counteract the earlier failures. In this way more and more men and resources were pushed in piece by piece until the battle took on a priority of its own, quite divorced from the actual value of the supposed target.

Prestige and stubbornness became the reason for the battle to continue, not the capture of Stalingrad itself.

It would not be the first time such a thing had happened. The great battle of Gettysburg that decided the American Civil War was another example. A Confederate regiment had gone to the town to capture a shoe factory, because they were short on footwear. Before they could get the shoes they were driven out by a Unionist division. The Confederates called up reinforcements and counterattacked, causing the Unionists to summon their own support. Before long the two main armies were locked in a deadly combat that neither had foreseen and neither wanted. It seems that much the same thing happened at Stalingrad.

When he received the orders of 23 July, Hoth was heading for Kalach, well on his way to Stalingrad. He then turned south towards the lower Don, to get behind the Soviets opposing Kleist. However, Timoshenko had ordered his men to fall back and to abandon the Don entirely. By the time Hoth arrived there were not only no Soviets to surround, but no Soviets to fight either.

Instead he found himself running into Kleist's panzers as they fanned out along the Don, seeking an intact bridge or a useable ford. Kleist was furious. Writing after the war, he said:

'The 4th Panzer Army was advancing on that line, on my left. It could have taken Stalingrad without a fight at the end of July, but was diverted south to help me in crossing the Don. I did not need its aid, and it merely congested the roads I was using. When it turned north again, a fortnight later, the Russians had gathered sufficient forces at Stalingrad to check it.'

In fact Kleist had pushed infantry and armoured cars over the river on 25 July and by the time Hoth arrived he had his engineers busily building or repairing bridges. The first panzers crossed on 27 July. On 29 July Hoth received fresh orders. He was to leave the 16th Motorized Division at Elista to cover the gap between the two panzer armies, then take the majority of his forces north to attack Stalingrad from the south while Paulus and his 6th Army attacked from the west.

The race for the oilfields

While Hoth turned north for Stalingrad, Army Group A pushed on towards its goal of capturing the oilfields, with Kleist and his panzers leading the way. Superficially his task was going to be straightforward. The lands in front of him were wide open and ideal for tank warfare. Moreover the Soviet forces, once driven out of Rostov, hardly put up any resistance at all. The pace of the advance quickened. On 29 July he took Proletarskaya, on 31 July Salsk, on 5 August Stavropol, on 7 August Armavir and on 9 August he entered the oilfields at Maikop. The Russians had, of course, smashed as much of the oil drilling and refining equipment as they could, but it would be only a matter of a few weeks before the German engineers got things going again.

In reality, the task set for Kleist was being changed in such a way that it would become effectively impossible. The same set of orders that had first mentioned the capture of Stalingrad had also widened the scope of the southern advance. Hitler now wanted List's Army Group A to capture not only the oilfields, but all of the Caucasus down to the Turkish and Persian borders and east to the Caspian Sea. This was a much increased task for List, more so than it appears on a map. He had been intending to seize the oilfields and then secure his conquests by driving the Russians into the hills and mountains to face a winter of hunger without ammunition. Now he would have to pursue them into the mountains, which was going to be a very tough campaign.

Not only had List been given a greatly increased task, but the tools with which he could achieve it were being taken away from him. Manstein and his 11th Army were sent north to join the siege of Leningrad. Just as bad, two of the best panzergrenadier (motorized infantry) divisions were also to leave Army Group A later in August. On 19 August an Allied raid on the French port of Dieppe had been made in strength with tanks, artillery and massive naval and air support. The raid had been repulsed with heavy losses, but Rundstedt, now in command in France, feared it would be the first in a series of such raids. Hitler agreed and sent him the two panzergrenadier divisions to bolster the defences of the western seaboard.

Walter Warlimont, deputy head of the OKW at the time, was scathing about this decision after the war.

'Hitler often underestimated the Russians. The worst mistake of this kind happened in August 1942 when, on account of the landings at Dieppe, Hitler lost his nerve. He gave the order that the SS-Leibstandarte and the Gross Deutschland divisions were to be transferred to the West. In spite of the objections of Halder (head of OKH) and Jodl (head of operations at OKW), Hitler insisted on his order. Only the Leibstandarte ever actually reached the Western Theatre. The Gross Deutschland was still in Russia when it was diverted again to Army Group Centre. It was a great failure.'

List objected to Halder, who passed on List's misgivings to Hitler. But once again, Hitler would not listen. He replied that the 8th Italian Army, the 2nd Hungarian Army and the 3rd and 4th Romanian Armies were going southeast to join the campaign, which more than made up for the units he had removed. On paper this was true, but these allied units were seriously deficient in both equipment and training. In particular they had little artillery, and almost no specialized anti-tank guns. The German senior generals were well aware of these weaknesses, so to set their minds at rest Hitler promised that the elite German 6th Army would hold the land bridge between the Don and the Volga. The allies would be asked to hold only the river lines where they had the additional advantage of strong natural defences to their front. Not only that but some German units would be put in reserve behind them to plug any gaps that emerged.

The drive to Stalingrad

Fatally, things did not work out as Hitler had planned. While Hoth and his 1st Panzer Army was on its fruitless drive south to Rostov, the 6th Army was hurrying forward as fast as it could. With his infantry, Paulus was not performing the task of racing ahead that should have been carried out by Hoth, while his own task of clearing out pockets of resistance was passed down to the Romanians, whose mission should have been merely to hold the defensive line established by the 6th Army. The results would be fatal.

As it hurried on down the Don, the 6th Army left behind it several small pockets of Russians on the south bank. These areas were isolated in convoluted bends and contained only small numbers of Red Army soldiers, who had been beaten back and shattered by the German drive. Paulus felt that he could ignore them in his rush to reach the Volga and Stalingrad. In the standard blitzkrieg pattern, such pockets would have been eliminated by the following infantry. But now the Romanians were the following infantry, and their orders had not changed. They were still simply told to dig in and fortify the lines left to them by the Germans. So the Soviet pockets on the south bank of the Don remained.

Paulus's men were getting tired, because of the constant marching. The Russian resistance was as weak as that being encountered by Kleist in the south, but the occasional Soviet rearguard actions, fought at small towns along the way, forced the Germans to deploy from the march to battle order and back again with exhausting frequency. The need to push on at speed meant that all too often the various units were not back in proper marching order before moving on, making the next deployment all the more confusing and irritating. By the time the 6th Army crossed the Don where it bent to the south, the army was in a highly disoriented order and in no state to fight a major battle.

On 25 July Paulus was over the Don. He decided to try to reach Stalingrad without first waiting to reorganize his scattered 6th Army, so he sent his divisions forward as they arrived. But for the first time the Soviet soldiers were dug in and fighting hard. After four days, Paulus called off the assault in order to wait until Hoth and his panzers arrived. Hoth was in position by 14 August, and the major offensive to capture Stalingrad, seize the south bank of the Volga and start the drive to Astrakhan was scheduled to begin on 19 August.

Meanwhile, in the south, Kleist was mad with rage. Throughout his long, fast drive to the oilfields he had been assisted by the 8th *Luftwaffe* Corps. The aircraft had been invaluable. Reconnaissance aircraft had flown far ahead of the panzers, locating Soviet forces and discovering which bridges were intact and which roads were clear of obstructions. The bombers, especially the Stukas, had attacked any Soviet strongpoints, clearing a path through which the panzers could advance at speed and without loss. The fighters had swarmed through the skies, knocking down any Soviet aircraft that dared take to the air. The unit was commanded by Wolfram Freiherr von Richthofen, a cousin of the famous Red Baron of the First World War, who insisted on a high standard of training in army co-operation for his men.

Now Richthofen and his aircraft were taken away

from Kleist and sent north to join the new offensive against Stalingrad. Speaking after the war, Kleist said:

'The ultimate cause of failure was that my forces were drawn away bit by bit to help the attack on Stalingrad. Besides part of my motorized infantry, I had to give up the whole of my flak corps and all my air force, apart from the reconnaissance squadrons. That subtraction contributed to what, in my opinion, was a further cause of the failure. The Russians suddenly concentrated a force of 800 bombers on my front, operating from airfields near Grozny. Although only about a third of these bombers were any good, they sufficed to put a brake on my advance, and it was all the more effective because of my lack of flak and fighters.'

Kleist's problems were serious, and getting worse. But they were as nothing compared to what was about to happen to Paulus and Hoth at Stalingrad.

5
INTO STALINGRAD

As the Germans' push towards Stalingrad got under way, they rapidly lost what had until then been one of their key advantages in the war against Russia. The war to date had been characterized by sweeping German advances led by panzer units that moved rapidly and – so far as the Soviets were concerned – unexpectedly. A panzer division might be heading northeast in the morning, only to change direction at lunchtime to race southeast and smash a Russian force that had been expecting a quiet afternoon. The flexibility of the German advance worked on a greater scale as well. The 600,000 Soviets captured at Vyazma were as much the result of German changes of direction as they were of firepower.

Lost advantages

In the early stages of the 1942 campaign, the Russians had reacted cautiously to the German advance because they knew that the panzers could change direction without warning. This was why Stalin insisted on keeping his main reserves near Moscow and why Vatutin was so eager to recapture and then hold on to Voronezh. By keeping the Soviet forces dispersed, the Germans made their own task much easier. They could strike through weakly held sectors of the front, surround strongly held areas and then move on to repeat the process. The Soviet commanders were unable to use their superior numbers to good effect. The Germans could choose when and where to attack, massing their units at the key point – the *Schwerpunkt* as they called it – to achieve an overwhelming superiority of numbers and fire power at the section where it mattered most.

But as it became increasingly clear that the offensive was being aimed at Stalingrad, all of these advantages were lost. Instead of the Soviets keeping their reserves dispersed to cover the various choices open to the advancing Germans, they could now concentrate their reserves and strength in the path that the Germans were bound to follow. Given Stalingrad's position on the Volga, with the Don only 64 kilometres (40 miles) to the west, the scope for manoeuvre open to the Germans was increasingly restricted as they got closer to the city.

Each attack carried the German forces closer to the city, but at heavier cost and for less gain. The Germans now found it impossible to break a gap through the Russian defences through which the motorized units could pour. This was not a style of fighting for which the Germans were either equipped or trained. The rather more old-fashioned Red Army was better suited to these blunt battering ram attacks than were the Germans. And things were only going to get worse.

There was another major disadvantage confronting the Germans as they pushed forward to Stalingrad, though they were slow to appreciate it. In a panzer blitzkrieg the main military strength was concentrated at the tip of the advance. It was here that the powerful tanks were needed to blast the opposition forces to pieces, smash through defensive positions and spread destruction as widely as possible. Behind this armoured fist stretched a long arm composed of less effective infantry and artillery units. There had always been a worry among the more conventionally-minded generals that if the fist got too far ahead of the arm it would be surrounded and destroyed. Such worries had surfaced during the occupation of Poland, and more seriously during the invasion of France, when more than once the panzers were brought to a temporary halt. In practice, though, so long as the armoured units in the fist kept moving, and the enemy was given no chance to reform or organize, there was no danger of being cut off.

But in the slow advance towards Stalingrad the armoured fist was not keeping on the move, nor were the Soviets denied the chance to concentrate and organize. Back in 1939 the situation would have caused concern at the OKH, though perhaps not so much among the troops pushing forward. By 1942 the situation was different. The generals had become accustomed to armoured spearheads being safe from flank attacks and so were slow to realize the danger. Perhaps more important was the fact that Hitler had by this date sacked most of the more conventional officers at the OKH and the OKW, and had cowed into subservience those that were left in position.

'Not One Step Backwards'

Meanwhile, the Soviet approach to defending Stalingrad was hardening. On 22 July Stalin and his chief of staff, Marshal Aleksandr Vasilevsky, had drawn up General Order No. 227 of the Stavka. This was later to become known as the 'Not One Step Backwards' order and was a truly terrifying piece of military discipline. After a preamble outlining the course of the war to date, the order got down to business.

'There is no order and discipline in companies, battalions, regiments, in tank units and air

squadrons. This is our main deficiency. We should establish in our army the most stringent order and solid discipline, if we want to salvage the situation, and to keep our Motherland. It is impossible to tolerate commanders and commissars permitting units to leave their positions. It is impossible to tolerate commanders and commissars who admit that some panic-mongers determined the situation on the field of combat and carried away in departure other soldiers and opened the front to the enemy. The panic-mongers and cowards should be exterminated in place. Henceforth the solid law of discipline for each commander, Red Army soldier, and commissar should be the requirement – not a single step back without order from higher command.

'Therefore all army commanders should;

'a) Unconditionally remove from their offices corps and army commanders and commissars who

have accepted troop withdrawals from occupied positions without the order of the army command, and route them to the military councils of the fronts for court martial;

'b) Form within the limits of each army 3 to 5 well-armed defensive squads (up to 200 persons in each), and put them directly behind unstable divisions and require them in case of panic and scattered withdrawals of elements of the divisions to shoot in place panic-mongers and cowards and thus help the honest soldiers of the division execute their duty to the Motherland;

'c) Form within the limits of each army up to ten (depending on the situation) penal companies (from 150 to 200 persons in each) into which will be put ordinary soldiers and low-ranking commanders who have been guilty of a breach of discipline due to cowardice or bewilderment, and put them at difficult sectors of the army to give them an opportunity to redeem by blood their crimes against the Motherland.'

The implementation of this order would prove to be extremely bloody. Whenever an attack was ordered, there would be a 'defensive squad' armed with machine-guns or a tank placed just behind the assaulting unit. Any man seen turning back would be shot dead and if the unit was deemed to be attacking with insufficient vigour the defensive squad would open fire.

It was not at all unusual for a unit of the Red Army to find itself machine-gunned by the Germans from the front and by their own comrades from behind. On occasion entire battalions were wiped out in this way.

Nor did the slaughter stop there. With both officers and men knowing that they would be shot out of hand if they showed any sign that could be interpreted as cowardice, orders to attack could not be questioned, still less disobeyed. During the drive to Stalingrad one German unit found itself being attacked by a Soviet regiment whose troops stormed forward without firing their guns. The Germans mowed down the hapless Russians by the hundred. Afterwards some of the less badly wounded were pulled in for questioning. It transpired that the men had not fired their guns since they had been sent into the attack without any ammunition. The German officer who wrote up the report expressed his amazement and disgust that the Russians could throw away their men's lives in such a brutal and pointless way.

The penal companies proved to be another method by which the Soviets inflicted heavy casualties on themselves. Many senior commanders took the view that the men who were sent to the penal companies were lucky not to have been shot and so gave them near-suicidal missions. Some were put to work digging anti-tank ditches under the guns of the approaching panzers. Others had the task of clearing German minefields by marching across them to set the mines off. Unsurprisingly, casualty rates were astonishingly high and in many cases reached 100 per cent in just a few days. In all, 422,000 men of the Red Army were sent to the punishment companies. Later in the war, the Soviets would empty prisons and send the inmates to the front to serve, and die, in punishment companies. An estimated 850,000 civilians died in this way.

The enthusiasm with which the NKVD (People's Commissariat for Internal Affairs) carried out Stalin's orders to stamp out cowardice and destroy spies went even further. Each Soviet division had attached to its headquarters a force of 20 NKVD officers and 30 NKVD men led by a senior NKVD officer. This unit was expected to build up a network of informers through the division, using them to crack down on defeatist talk, anti-Communist activity and cowardice. They had the right to try and execute any member of the division without reference to the general officer commanding. NKVD officers were under intense pressure to root out cowardice and defeatism, so many expressed their zeal through the numbers of men they executed.

Fortress Stalingrad

The Soviet civilians also began to suffer. The evacuation of the city, a usual practice when Germans were approaching, was halted. Instead the civilians were organized into 'worker's units', based on where they lived, and marched out of the city. There they were given shovels, picks and other tools and ordered to help the army prepare its defences. Tank ditches 1.8 metres (six feet) deep were dug to halt the dreaded panzers. Buildings and trees were removed to give the anti-tank guns clear fields of fire. Trees were felled and sawn up to be built into bunkers and gun emplacements. The rations given to the workers' units were basic in the extreme, and hunger and sickness were common. Moreover the NKVD had commandeered all of the boats on the Volga for its own purposes, making the evacuation of children and the elderly impossible. About 400,000 civilians were still in the city.

By this date there had been a change of command in the Red Army. Timoshenko had been moved north to a quiet sector of the line, to be replaced by Andrey Yeremenko. The city's civil administration was put into the hands of Nikita Khrushchev, who had narrowly escaped capture at Kiev. Together the two men began planning the defence of the city. As well as the static defences around Stalingrad, they began converting the city itself into a fortified base. Some streets were barricaded to block them to German vehicles, while others were left open to lure the Germans forward into carefully prepared ambushes.

Houses and factories were gutted so they could be converted into machine-gun nests and anti-tank gun emplacements. Holes were made in the walls between houses, often in the attics or the cellars, so that men could move easily from one house to the next, travelling from one end or side of a street to the other without actually emerging into the street at all.

The attack begins

On 19 August 1942 their time ran out. The Germans were on the move.

Two German armies were involved in the drive to Stalingrad. The first was the 6th Army under Paulus, the second the 4th Panzer Army under Hoth. Although the panzers would be expected to provide the main offensive punch, Paulus was the more senior general, so the operation came under his command. Paulus was operating under the overall control of Weichs at Army Group B, and all were answerable to the OKH and so to Hitler. Right from the start Hitler interfered. When things had been going well in the first three years of the war he had been content to decide on the broad sweep of strategy and leave his generals to get on with the detailed tactics. That was how the German military system was supposed to operate, with the man on the spot deciding how best to achieve the aims set for him with the resources at his disposal.

But with radio sets allowing instant access to information and orders, Hitler was able to learn about tactical deployments at a regimental level. And as the tide of war turned against Germany he was increasingly inclined to get involved in the detailed tactical decisions. This drove his generals to distraction. In a situation where Hitler had an interest he would interfere constantly, but in other areas he would put off making decisions because he did not have the time – and so crucial opportunities were lost and mistakes were made. The Stalingrad campaign would demonstrate both aspects of Hitler's increasingly tight control of military matters – and the trend was only going to get worse.

The plan that emerged from Paulus was for a conventional offensive against a prepared defence. In his centre he placed the nine infantry divisions of the 6th Army. On his northern flank he put three panzer and two motorized infantry divisions. On the southern flank he positioned two panzer and two motorized divisions. He had a preponderance of strength. The Soviets had about 50,000 men on the west bank of the Volga: Paulus had at least twice as many men in position.

The Soviet position to be assaulted was some 80 kilometres (50 miles) across, but as it bowed forward towards the Germans it measured 129 kilometres (80 miles) along the actual front. The left, or southern end, of the line rested on the Volga, the right on the Don. Inside this defensive half ring were the 62nd Army and the 64th Army, plus an assortment of odd brigades and divisions that had retreated back towards Stalingrad as the German advance had rolled down the Don valley.

The Soviet forces in the area were under the command of Andrey Yeremenko, but it was not long before Stalin followed his usual practice of sending a trusted commander to a point of crisis, to take temporary control. In this instance he chose to send Georgy Zhukov, who had organized the defence of Moscow the previous winter and had since divided his time between Moscow and sectors of the front in the north. With him Zhukov brought the artillery specialist Nikolai Voronov and the air commander Novikov. Zhukov's firm and ruthless hand would be clearly visible in much of what was to follow.

The German attack soon ran into problems, particularly the panzers on the southern side near Lake Sarpa. Both the Soviets and the German general officers put the blame on cautious behaviour by the frontline troops, especially the panzers. Many men believed that the war was almost over. There seems to have been a reluctance to run risks that might prove fatal when everyone might be going home to their families in a few weeks' time. There was also the fact that Hitler had ordered Hoth to divert one of his three corps south to the Caucasus. Whatever the reason for the slow start, the Germans soon got into their stride.

The key breakthrough was made by the XIV Panzer Corps commanded by General Gustav von Wietersheim. Operating on the far left of the German line, Wietersheim punched through the Soviet defences and drove fast across the gently undulating grasslands in front of them. By dusk he was into the northern suburbs of Stalingrad. Next day Wietersheim's lead unit, the 16th Panzer Division of General Hans-Valentine Hube, reached the Volga River north of the city. The panzer guns dominated the vast mile-wide river, sinking seven barges or other craft in the first few hours. One of the ships sunk was a ferry carrying women and children to safety on the east bank. The Germans ceased fire to allow the Russians to mount a rescue effort. It was a rare incident of chivalry on the Eastern Front.

Hurrying up into the breach created by the panzers

came the infantry and artillery of the 51st Corps, one of four in the 6th Army. The corps was commanded by General Walther von Seydlitz, a member of one of the most famous military families in Germany. As the infantry appeared on the banks of the Volga, Paulus believed his plan was coming to fruition and that the city would soon be his.

In order to clear the way into the city, Paulus turned to Richthofen and asked him to pound the city and its defences. The raid proved to be the largest of the war so far. Richthofen not only used his entire 4th *Luftwaffe* Corps, but also called on as many long-range bombers as could reach the city. He was keen to finish this campaign as quickly as possible. His men had been flying a succession of low-level missions to attack Soviet tanks. It was exhausting and dangerous work, very different from the sort of tactical bombing for which the *Luftwaffe* crews had been trained. Even his fighters had been ordered into ground attack missions. If Stalingrad could be taken quickly, Richthofen's men would return to less hazardous work. In all 1,200 aircraft took part in the great raid on Stalingrad, some of them flying two or even three sorties.

The bomb loads dropped on Stalingrad were half high explosive and half incendiary. It was a deadly mix. The explosives destroyed or damaged buildings, smashing windows, blasting off tiles and toppling walls. Then the incendiaries came to set fire to the roof timbers and floor planks exposed by the explosives. House after house, factory after factory, apartment block after apartment block went up in flames. Those untouched by the blasts were often consumed by fires spreading from neighbouring buildings. A vast cloud of smoke towered up from the burning city. Night fell and a German officer recorded in his diary that he could read his newspaper by the light of flaming Stalingrad – and he was 48 kilometres (30 miles) distant.

A state of siege

The widespread destruction visited on Stalingrad had no influence on the fighting raging around it. The German advances continued, but progress was painfully slow. But combined with Wietersheim's breakthrough to the Volga it did have an effect on Stalin. The Stalingrad Party Committee was instructed to declare a state of siege in the city. Posters carrying the declaration went up everywhere:

'Dear comrades! Stalingrad citizens! Our city is experiencing hard days, just like we did 24 years ago. Bloody Hitlerites have torn their way to sunny Stalingrad and to the great river Volga. Stalingrad citizens! Let us not allow the Germans to desecrate our native city. Let us rise as one to protect our beloved city, homes, and families. Please leave your homes and build impregnable barricades on every street. Let us make each quarter, each house, each street an unassailable fortress. We will emulate our great fathers of 1918 who defended Tsaritsyn and live up to our award of the Order of the Red Banner of Stalingrad! Everyone to the barricades! All those who can carry a rifle must protect their native city and homes!'

It was not just a matter of putting up posters. Such evacuation of women, children and the elderly that had been taking place was halted. Factory managers were ordered to stop the dismantling of machinery for shipment to safety. Instead all equipment was to stay in the city, together with all of the civilians. Stalin wanted to halt any moves that made it look as if the Red Army so much as contemplated losing Stalingrad to the Germans. The NKVD was given the task of stopping anyone from leaving the city, a task they carried out using murderous methods.

The NKVD was also put in charge of organizing all adult civilians into 'Worker Militia Battalions'. Men and women working in Stalingrad's armaments factories were at first excused from serving in the Worker Militia, but that would later change. The NKVD cared little for the welfare of its new recruits. One Worker Militia Battalion was sent to counterattack the 16th Panzer Division in the north, although some 20 per cent of the men had no weapons. They were simply told to pick up the guns dropped by their comrades as they were killed. Casualties were huge among the Russians, the effect on the panzers minimal. Indeed, the Germans managed a small advance that yielded huge benefits, when they captured an entire trainload of American equipment sent to help the Red Army. Officers gleefully commandeered American Jeeps to replace the Volkswagen staff cars that they had been using so far.

Closing the ring

On 27 August it rained heavily. As usual this brought about a sudden, but temporary lull in the fighting as the roads turned to mush. Hoth used the enforced delay to study the map, take careful stock of the situation and assess Soviet dispositions. Two days later the ground was dry and he struck. This time he smashed a hole in the Soviet lines and began a drive for the Volga. At one point it looked as if his panzers might get behind the Soviet 64th Army and trap them completely. Yeremenko moved too fast, however, and issued orders for an emergency retreat back to the suburbs.

In the north, the Soviets were assembling three armies to launch a counterattack on Wietersheim's panzers and drive them away from the Volga. The 24th and 66th Armies and the 1st Guards Army were moving up around Frolovo, north of the Don. On 29 August Zhukov arrived to oversee the assault and was appalled by what he found. The three armies were short on artillery and tanks, had a disproportionate number of old reservists and were, in any case, hopelessly disorganized after their journey to the front by train. The poor state of morale was demonstrated by the 64th Division, which had broken and fled when caught in the open by German aircraft. Once he had got his men back together, the general commanding put them on parade, loaded his pistol and shot a dozen of them dead on the spot. Zhukov phoned the Stavka and persuaded Stalin to give him time to get things organized before the attack began.

On 3 September a renewed, albeit minor, German advance by Hoth finally closed the ring around Stalingrad. Panzers now stood on the banks of the

Volga south of the city as well as north. Paulus was delighted and wrote out a self-congratulatory telegram to be sent to Weichs at Army Group HQ and to Hitler.

The same news led to Zhukov being called to the telephone to speak to an angry Stalin, who ordered him to attack at once regardless of the state of the assaulting forces. 'Delay,' raged Stalin, 'is the equivalent of a crime.' Zhukov kept his nerve and gained 48 hours delay. When the attack was made against the elite panzer corps holding the northern flank of Paulus's line, it proved to be a failure. The Russians ended the offensive where it had begun. The Germans claimed that they had taken 26,500 prisoners and destroyed 350 guns and 830 tanks, and had inflicted huge but unspecified casualties.

Discussing strategy

Zhukov was back where he had started, but with considerably fewer men. He seems to have now accepted that attacks on the Germans were pointless.

Instead he decided to defend Stalingrad by feeding in just enough men each day to replace losses and to stop a complete collapse of the defence. He would lure the Germans into a siege fought in the urban streets, where their more sophisticated artillery and panzers would lose the advantage that they had enjoyed out in the open countryside, where they had won most of their spectacular victories. If he had only known it, Zhukov had chosen exactly the correct strategy. Paulus was devising a plan that played straight into Zhukov's hands.

On 12 September Paulus and Weichs were summoned to a meeting with Hitler to explain their plans in detail and to hear what Hitler thought of them. The generals travelled west by train to reach Hitler's new forward headquarters complex codenamed 'Werewolf', which had been built near the Ukrainian town of Vinnitsa. The heavily defended command centre consisted mostly of stoutly-built wooden houses, though there was a large concrete bunker deep underground as protection against any bombing raids the Russians might attempt. While gaining entrance to the areas where the staff officers toiled was relatively straightforward, Hitler's Führer House had only one narrow door at which sat an SS officer, day and night. Nobody was allowed in with a weapon or without a special pass. The inner complex included a small but intensively worked horticultural garden, so that Hitler could enjoy his favourite varieties of fruit and vegetables, picked fresh on the day they were served.

On their arrival, Paulus and Weichs were welcomed by Halder, then ushered in to meet Hitler. The official records of the meeting were later lost, but according to Paulus the meeting began with Hitler outlining the latest intelligence reports on the state of the Red Army and the Soviet Union. These, Hitler said, showed that the Soviet Union was reaching the end of its endurance. Resources of men and *matériel* were both running out and although the Red Army could be expected to hurl more men and tanks into counterattacks, these were the last gambles of a collapsing regime. There then followed a much shorter briefing on the progress of fighting on other fronts such as Leningrad – where all was well according to Hitler.

Then came the in-depth discussion of Stalingrad. Paulus explained his plan. He was going to send two columns of attackers into the southern half of the city with the aim of capturing the main ferry terminals, through which the Russians were bringing reinforcements and supplies into the besieged city. The more southerly column was the stronger of the two. It was to form up in the suburb of Yelshanka then head northeast into the city. This force was composed of the 94th Infantry Division and the 29th Motorized Division, with the 14th and 24th Panzer Divisions providing tank and self-propelled artillery support. The northern force was made up of the 71st, 76th and 295th Infantry Divisions. It was to advance almost due east from Gumrak with Red Square in the city centre as its primary objective. Once the ferry terminal and the adjacent areas were in his hands, Paulus said, the remaining Soviet forces in Stalingrad would have no means of supply and would be forced to surrender.

Hitler asked Paulus how long the operation would take. According to Halder (Paulus later disputed his account), Paulus replied that it would take 10 days to capture the ferry terminals and the surrounding city sections, then another 14 to 16 days to clear the rest of the city. Hitler declared that 'The vital thing now is to concentrate every available man and capture as quickly as possible the whole of Stalingrad and the banks of the Volga to the Caspian.' He then told Paulus that he was being given three fresh infantry divisions that would start arriving in the Stalingrad area by 18 September.

Paulus later claimed that he then raised the question of the forces protecting his flanks and rear (Halder says he did not). Hitler brushed aside the question by asserting that the allied armies from Italy, Romania and Hungary could easily take care of the defence of the flanks. They were, he said, better equipped than they had been and were supported by German units held in reserve. In any case, Hitler repeated, the Soviets were in no position to mount a major offensive at Stalingrad.

Underestimating the enemy

In fact, the OKH intelligence estimation of Soviet power was neither as clear-cut nor as accurate as Hitler had led Paulus and Weichs to believe. The intelligence reports arriving at the OKH indicated that the Soviets had been able to step up their production of tanks, aircraft and guns. Of particular concern to the Germans was the Ilyushin Shturmovik, a ground attack aircraft armed with eight 82 mm rockets that were capable of knocking out a panzer. The aircraft was first used just before the German invasion in 1941 and by the summer of 1942 it was beginning to enter service in large numbers. The Soviets would eventually build 36,000 examples of the Shturmovik.

The other big concern was the improved T34 tank, also being manufactured in large numbers. One of the factories producing the T34 was located in Stalingrad. The factory continued to manufacture tanks as the battle progressed, with T34s being driven off the production line and straight into battle. Exactly how many of these new weapons, and existing models, the

Soviets were producing was a matter of heated debate in German intelligence circles. Certainly the numbers were higher than German production of similar weapons, but many – including Hitler – constantly underestimated Soviet manufacturing capacity.

The OKH was also aware that the Red Army was actually expanding at this date. Again, there was much dispute in German circles as to how quickly and effectively the Red Army was growing. Reports from the front line continued to highlight the poor quality of Russian soldiers, their training and their officers. There was, however, one thing about which the German high command was united in its belief and that was where the Soviets were massing for their next offensive.

Falling into the Soviet trap

Since the failure of the German drive on Moscow, and the Soviet counterattack, the central area of the Eastern Front had been largely inactive. Both sides had constructed large-scale static defences there, including trench systems, dugouts and command bunkers, that had more in common with the First World War than the Second. The Germans used this quiet area to rest divisions and units that had been involved in heavy fighting elsewhere.

The Soviets, however, used the same quiet sector as a first posting for new and inexperienced units. The Germans had, of course, noted the presence of these new units, which usually had better and more up-to-date equipment than the older units. The Germans saw a succession of Soviet units arrive in the line north of Kursk, stay for a few weeks and then move away again. Believing the Soviets were doing what they would do in similar circumstances, the Germans concluded that the Red Army was giving the units experience of a sector where they would soon be launching an offensive. Once they had spent a short time in the front line, the Germans believed, these units were moved into reserve behind the same sector.

Thus the Germans had, by September 1942, concluded that the Soviets were planning to launch a major offensive somewhere around Briansk or

Smolensk. Given the fate of similar Soviet offensives –
including that launched by Zhukov near Stalingrad on
the orders of Stalin – the Germans believed that Army
Group Centre was perfectly capable of defeating, or at
least limiting, such an offensive. Almost certainly Hitler
and the OKH were correct in anticipating a victory for
Army Group Centre which, with two panzer armies
and two infantry armies, was strong enough to defend
its positions.

However, the Soviets were not massing to attack
there at all. As soon as a unit had gained some
battle experience it was moved away from the Army
Group Centre area to join the general reserve of the
Red Army. From there the unit could be used almost
anywhere that Stalin desired. What the Germans had
interpreted as being preparations for a major offensive
in the central area during the winter were nothing of
the kind.

As Weichs and Paulus left Werewolf to return to
their respective headquarters, there was one aspect
of the meeting about which nobody had commented.

For the initial offensive into the Soviet Union, and ever since, Hitler had insisted that orders always emphasized the importance of not getting drawn into street fighting in urban areas.

Hitler and his generals had appreciated that the Germans' weapons and tactics gave them a great advantage when it came to fast-moving, mobile battles fought in open country, but in static, close-quarters city fighting they would have no such advantage. It was for this reason that, quite rightly, Hitler and his high command had insisted on bypassing cities and towns. And yet Hitler had now agreed to a senior general's plan that called for the Germans to fight a static, city battle.

Already the lure of the mighty city of Stalingrad, with its key strategic position and its name, had got the better of the German planners. Stalingrad was not worth the risks that were being run to capture it.

Chuikov

As chance would have it, the Soviets held a conference the day after Paulus and Weichs met with Hitler and

Halder. This time it was Vasily Chuikov, commander of the 64th Army, who had been summoned to head-quarters. There he met Yeremenko and Khrushchev. The two senior men began by outlining the military situation concerning the 62nd Army, then isolated in the city centre. They emphasized that there could be no surrender, no escape and little by way of reinforcements. They then told Chuikov that they needed a new commander for the 62nd Army and that they wanted Chuikov, but first they had to ask him a question.

'Comrade Chuikov,' said Khrushchev, 'how do you interpret the task facing the new commander of the 62nd Army?'

Chuikov glanced once more at the map of the city, then said, 'To defend Stalingrad or to die.'

'Correct,' said Yeremenko, who then handed Chuikov his appointment as commander of the trapped army. That night Chuikov crossed the Volga on a supply ferry carrying T34 tanks and artillery ammunition. He arrived just as the great offensive by Paulus was getting under way.

6
RATTENKRIEG

Even while Paulus and Weichs were travelling back from Werewolf, the offensive had begun. German artillery and bombers were pounding the Soviet front lines. Chuikov, in his command bunker, was covered in soil, which came trickling down from above. By mid-afternoon all of his telephone links to his units, and to Yeremenko on the east bank of the Volga, had been cut. Men sent out to repair them had been killed and the lines had been cut again. After dusk he abandoned his bunker and moved to a much deeper old tunnel that ran from the Tsaritsa Gorge to the banks of the Volga. It was further underground, though not so conveniently situated.

Street fighting men

At 6.45 am the ground assault got under way, the artillery and bomber barrage continuing but shifting east, to avoid any accidental strikes on the German troops. The 295th Division, spearheading the northern column, hoped to reach the Volga before nightfall. It was not to be. The Russian resistance was stronger than expected and the Germans very quickly found that their training in street fighting had not prepared them for the grim reality. Accustomed to advancing miles each day, they now counted their progress in metres. By dusk on 13 September the soldiers of the division had fought their way to the eastern side of the great open park called the Mamayev Kurgan. Their companions in the 71st Division had veered south and were approaching the lip of the Tsaritsa Gorge.

At Werewolf the mood was jubilant. The attack was going to plan and progress was good if unspectacular. Zhukov was in Moscow briefing Stalin on the situation when a phone call from Yeremenko gave them the news of the German advance. Zhukov raced from the room to board a plane heading south while Stalin ordered an extra division, the 13th Guards, to cross the river into the city.

Before dawn on 14 September, Chuikov launched a counterattack to press in on the flanks of the advancing Germans. The assault made painfully slow progress, though it did cause the Germans to halt their advance for a few hours. Then the Stukas came and with impressive accuracy pounded the houses where the Soviets were. By mid-morning Chuikov had lost all of his gains and the German advance had begun again. At 11 am the Germans captured the main Stalingrad railway station, then half an hour later the Russians recaptured it, only to lose it again by 1 pm and retake it by 5 pm. By that time Chuikov had deployed his final reserves – a squad of 19 tanks – and he had nothing left to use.

At this stage in the attack on Stalingrad, the Germans were using the same urban tactics that had stood them in good stead during the limited amounts of street fighting in which they had been involved to date. Each attacking group was made up of a company of soldiers (at full strength 80 men, though this was rarely the case) or sometimes two companies, plus a group of three or four panzers. Men's lives were valuable, and so were panzers, so an approach that cost the Germans the least of both was devised.

First the infantry would slowly infiltrate a street in order to identify enemy bunkers, strongpoints and occupied buildings. They were expected to keep a particularly sharp eye out for the location of any anti-tank weapons. Very often the enemy positions were located only when they opened fire on the infantry, for which reason this initial advance was usually slow, the men keeping close to cover whenever possible. Once the enemy positions had been located, the panzers would come up. The tanks would usually advance as a pair, with a third tank being held back to cover the rear. The lead tank would get into a position from where it could use its main gun to blast the enemy. The second tank would follow a short distance behind but hold its fire. Instead, its commander would continually scan the area for any hidden enemy positions that the infantry had not noticed, and especially for anti-tank weapons that might be a threat to the lead panzer. Only if any such were identified would the second tank open fire.

Panzers continued to carry some of their usual armour-piercing shells in case an enemy tank came into the combat area. However, for street fighting they were also equipped with more conventional artillery ammunition. Unlike armour-piercing shells, these exploded on impact, demolishing buildings and scattering lethal fragments in all directions.

Panzer crews preferred to stand back from the actual fighting and fire their shells into the combat zone. The main reason for this was that the rear upper deck of a panzer, behind the turret, was notoriously thinly armoured. In the usual run of open, fast-moving combat, for which the tanks had been designed, this was not much of a handicap. Most incoming rounds came at a low trajectory from the front. The chances of a falling shot coming from the rear were very slim. But in urban fighting such a shot was much more likely, especially if the tank ventured into a narrow street where missiles could be dropped on to it from the upper storeys of houses.

If any particularly strong defensive positions were encountered, both panzers and infantry would pull back while Stukas were called up to bomb the enemy. Then the ground advance would start again.

Inevitably, progress in urban fighting was slow. Each room in a building had to be cleared of the enemy, and each building in a street, before the street could be declared captured. Even if there were no Russians this was a process that could take a couple of hours. With the danger of instant death at any moment, the soldiers moved cautiously and slowly, as did the panzers. It was a nerve-wracking, terrifying style of fighting. The Germans called it '*Rattenkrieg*', or 'rat warfare'.

However, at this date the 6th Army was fresh into combat, close to full strength and confident of victory. The German attacks produced steady gains in terms of ground won and, although it is impossible to be certain, the Germans still seemed to suffer fewer casualties than the Russians.

The Soviet defenders were being squeezed mercilessly. Chuikov had only 80 tanks left, of which a third were unable to move, having been built into the defences as static artillery positions. Unlike the assaulting Germans, the defending Russian soldiers had mostly come from shattered units that had been defeated once already and had then retreated to Stalingrad. The local militia were poorly trained and badly armed. They were giving way along the entire 16-kilometre (ten-mile) front that remained to Chuikov.

Salvation for Chuikov came when a figure so covered in mud and dirt that his uniform could not be identified came staggering into his command tunnel. It was General Aleksandr Rodimtsev, commander of the 13th Guards Division, come to report that the first units of his 10,000 men were disembarking from the ferries and only awaited their artillery support before they went into action. On his way to Chuikov's command tunnel Rodimtsev had been forced to dive into craters and trenches on four occasions to avoid Stuka attacks. Chuikov told him there was no time for the artillery. His men would have to go into action with only their personal weapons. Rodimtsev hurried back outside to return to the ferry terminal and lead his men into the line against the German 71st Division.

Chuikov takes sole command

Chuikov then sent for Colonel A. Sarayev, head of the NKVD in Stalingrad. Sarayev had command of the 7,000 or so NKVD men in the city, plus the various Workers' Militia Battalions. As was usual in the Soviet Union, Sarayev owed allegiance to the NKVD, not to anyone else, and was answerable to the ferocious Lavrentiy Beria who had organized the purges for Stalin and was thought to have personally executed over a thousand people during his career. Chuikov told him that until the Germans had been defeated there could only be one commander in Stalingrad, that this man was going to be Chuikov and that Sarayev had better get used to obeying his orders.

The NKVD commander was aghast. Such a situation was unheard of in Russia. For an army officer to claim precedence over a Communist Party official struck at the foundation of the Soviet system. In any case, Beria had threatened only a year earlier to personally shoot any NKVD official who obeyed a military order without first getting authorization from NKVD headquarters. There was a tense silence lasting several seconds while the two men stared at each other. Then Sarayev snapped to attention and saluted.

It proved to be a crucial event. Chuikov was now indisputably in charge of all aspects of the defence of Stalingrad. With even the local NKVD obeying his commands, nobody else dared so much as question his orders. The defence of the city certainly needed a single command and a unified strategy. It was as well for the Soviets that Chuikov was a gifted defensive commander.

The event came not a moment too soon, for at around 3 pm on 14 September the Germans broke through the Russian defences. It was the 76th Division that had made the key breakthrough, powering in past the advances made by the 71st and 295th Divisions. One Russian officer recorded:

'Lorry loads of infantry and tanks raced into the city centre. The Germans must have thought that they had won Stalingrad already. They all rushed to the Volga as fast as they could and then began grabbing bits and pieces as souvenirs. I saw one group of Germans who looked drunk dancing about on the pavements while one of them played a tune on a mouth organ.'

The German advanced units were just 183 metres (200 yards) from Chuikov's command bunker. One heavy machine-gun was able to fire straight at the main ferry landing terminal where Rodimtsev's men were trying to get ashore. The ferries abandoned the terminal and instead began dropping the men off into the river to wade ashore. Bullets lanced into the water and casualties were heavy, but the 13th Guards kept on coming ashore.

As each unit landed, Rodimtsev pointed them in the direction they had to go and told them where to take up a defensive position alongside those already suffering the hammer blows of the Germans. 'Remember,' he shouted after each unit 'for us there is no land behind the Volga.' Within 24 hours 3,000 of his 10,000 men would be dead or wounded. But he was right. For Rodimtsev and all of his men, no matter how badly wounded, there was no prospect of going back over the Volga. If they were to live they had to drive the Germans out of Stalingrad.

The 13th Guards managed to halt the German advance and push back the few units that had reached the Volga. The ferry terminal was no longer under machine-gun fire and the inward flow of supplies, ammunition and men again gathered pace.

Mamayev Kurgan

On 15 September the focus of the fighting shifted to the Mamayev Kurgan park. This large open area was centred around a hill – actually a huge burial mound some 90 metres (300 feet) tall that had been built by the Tatars centuries earlier. The Germans wanted to secure the summit of the hill as an artillery position, from which they would be able to sweep the entire Volga, destroying any craft that attempted to cross. The hill had already been blasted by bombs and shells, so that all of the trees had been felled and the ground was pockmarked with craters. Now infantry and tanks moved in to capture the park. By dusk on 5 September most of Mamayev Kurgan park, including the crucial hill, was in German hands. A soldier of the 295th Division had been carrying a red, white and black Nazi Party flag with him throughout the campaign. Now it was tied to the branch of a fallen tree and erected on the summit of the hill.

The Russians launched a counterattack at dawn on 16 September. Men of the 13th Guards and an NKVD battalion pushed forward in the face of heavy fire to recapture part of the park. Towards nightfall the Russians launched an attack on the Mamayev Kurgan hill. They reached the summit where a man named Kentya of the 13th Guards kicked down the Nazi flag and stamped it into the mud. The German 295th Division then counterattacked themselves and regained the hill summit, but lost it again the following day. Back and forth the struggle raged over the following days as casualties mounted on both sides. In the end the battle for the hill ground to a halt on 27 September, with both sides holding part of the park, but neither able to hold the hill nor use it properly. By that time there was no grass left on the hill, so thoroughly had the ground been churned up by explosions and bullets. After the war a study found more than 1,000 splinters of metal in each square metre of soil.

The grain elevator

Meanwhile, the southern force of the Germans had been making steady progress towards the centre of the city. This area of Stalingrad had been composed largely of wooden houses, most of which had burned down after the major air raid some days earlier. The landscape here was an eerie one of charred timbers interspersed with brick chimneys standing like erect fingers.

Dominating the entire area was a massive concrete grain elevator that towered high into the sky, covered an entire city block and was so stoutly constructed that it was effectively impervious to artillery fire. The German advance lapped up and around the grain elevator, but inside the Russian soldiers still held out.

By the night of 17 September only 52 Soviets were left alive inside the grain elevator. Andrey Khozyaynov, a sailor who had been given a rifle and sent into the city to fight, was one of the defenders. He later wrote down his account of what had happened.

'I remember on the night of the 17th, I was called to the battalion command post and given the order to take a platoon of machine-gunners to the grain elevator and ... to hold it come what may. We arrived that night and presented ourselves to the garrison commander. At that time the elevator was being defended by a battalion of not more than 30 to 35 guardsmen. Eighteen well-armed men had now arrived from our platoon.

'At dawn enemy tanks and infantry, approximately ten times our numbers, launched an attack from the south and west. After the first attack was beaten back, a second began, then a third, while a reconnaissance plane circled over us. It corrected the fire and reported our position. In all, ten attacks were beaten off on 18 September.

'In the elevator, the grain was on fire, the cooling water in the machine-guns evaporated, the wounded were thirsty, but there was no water. This is how we defended ourselves 24 hours a day for three days. Heat, smoke, and thirst – all our lips were cracked. During the day many of us climbed up to the highest points in the elevator and from there fired on the Germans; at night we came down and made a defensive ring round the building. We had no contact with other units.

'20 September arrived. At noon 12 enemy tanks came up from the south and west. We had almost run out of ammunition for our anti-tank rifles, and we had no grenades left. The tanks approached the elevator from two sides and began to fire at our garrison at point-blank range. But no one flinched. Our machine-guns and tommy-guns continued to fire at the enemy's infantry, preventing them from entering the elevator. Then a Maxim, together with the gunner, was blown up by a shell, and the casing of the second Maxim was hit by shrapnel ... We were left with one light machine-gun.

'At dawn a German tank carrying a white flag approached from the south. We wondered what could have happened. Two men emerged from the tank, a Nazi officer and an interpreter. Through the interpreter the officer tried to persuade us to surrender to "the heroic German army", as defence was useless and we would not be able to hold our position any longer. "Better to surrender the elevator," affirmed the German officer. "If you refuse you will be dealt with without mercy. In an hour's time we will bomb you out of existence."

'"What impudence," we thought, and gave the Nazi lieutenant a brief answer: "Tell all your Nazis

---

*to go to hell! You can go back, but only on foot."
The German tank tried to beat a retreat, but a
salvo from our two anti-tank rifles stopped it.
The Germans made 10 attacks on the elevator, all
failed. As the grain burned, the cooling water in the
machine-guns evaporated, leaving all, especially the
wounded, thirsty. The explosions were shattering
the concrete; the grain was in flames. We could not
see one another for dust and smoke, but we cheered
one another with shouts. German tommy-gunners
appeared from behind the tanks. There were about
200 of them. They attacked very cautiously, throwing
grenades in front of them. We were able to catch
some of the grenades and throw them back. On the
west side of the elevator, the Germans managed to
enter the building, but we immediately turned our
guns on the parts they occupied. Fighting flared up
inside the building. We sensed and heard the enemy
soldiers' breath and footsteps, but we could not see
them in the smoke. We fired at the sound. At night,
during a short lull, we counted our ammunition.*

'There did not seem to be much left. We decided to break out. To begin with all went well. We passed through a gully and crossed a railroad line, then stumbled on an enemy mortar battery. The Germans scattered, leaving behind their weapons, but also bread and water. "Something to drink!" was all we could think about. We drank our fill in the darkness. We then ate the bread ... and went on.

'But alas, what happened to my comrades I don't know, because the next thing I remembered was waking in a dark, damp cellar. A door opened, and in the bright sunlight I could see a tommy-gunner in a black uniform. On his left sleeve was a skull. I had fallen into the hands of the enemy.'

What Khozyaynov nowhere reveals is that after he and his comrades had entered the grain elevator, the regimental commissar had ordered all the doors and windows to be bricked up so that the men inside could not get out.

The grain elevator was finally in German hands,

but in the southern sector as well as in the north the advance had ground to a halt. The attack had succeeded in reaching the Volga and capturing the Tsaritsa Gorge – thus forcing Chuikov to shift his command post for a second time – but it had run out of steam. The arrival of the 13th Guards had been just enough to save Stalingrad from falling during this first attack. Zhukov sent over the 284th Division to bolster the defence.

German worries

The extent to which contemporary observers could get some things correct and yet be mistaken about others is shown by a British report on the situation in Stalingrad, sent a few days after the September offensives came to an end. The report read:

'With von Bock concentrating the bulk of his forces on the Volga front and pressing his attack on Stalingrad regardless of cost, the situation by the middle of September had become more serious than ever. The Russian resistance

continued to be magnificent and the removal of shipping up the river was a sign that the battle would be fought out without thought of retreat.

'Von Bock's first drive against the city from the west looked at one time to succeed, but it was met by strong counterattacks and defeated. Then the attack from the Kotelnikov direction seemed to be most dangerous, but it was checked by stubborn Russian defences. The losses on both sides mounted at an appalling rate.'

The report gave a reasonably accurate, if brief account of the fighting, but it was wrong in one crucial respect. Bock had been removed from command almost two months earlier and yet word had not reached the Russians that he had gone. In war, secrecy is paramount and changes in the high command are no different. If a general with a reputation for skill in attacking is known by the enemy to have taken over a section of the front then they might conclude that an attack is imminent.

On 18 September Zhukov had attempted to relieve pressure on Chuikov's men by staging a limited offensive north of the city. The assault had failed, serving only to give the men of the 16th Panzer Division something to shoot at. The event did, however, have some serious repercussions.

General von Wietersheim had defeated the Soviet drive with ease, but had been worried nonetheless. The corridor held by the Germans that led to the Volga was narrow and the infantry had been unable to widen it. During the attack, Wietersheim's panzers had had only limited room in which to manoeuvre, which had hampered their preferred tactics for dealing with the T34 Soviet tanks. Moreover, Russian artillery fire had come in from both sides of the German-held corridor, ensuring that there was no safe area in the rear where German units could reform ready to renew an attack or support a defence.

Wietersheim was convinced that the area around Rynok was unsuitable for a defensive battle to be fought by panzers. Since his previous requests for reinforcements to attack, and so widen, the corridor had all been turned down, Wietersheim now suggested that his panzers should be withdrawn from the corridor for use elsewhere and that the Rynok area should be held by a reinforced infantry corps with artillery support. The request went to Paulus, who was furious. He accused Wietersheim of defeatism and recommended to Hitler that he be relieved of command. Within days Wietersheim had been moved to the ignoble position of commanding a group of supply trucks, a job far below his rank and experience. He was later dismissed completely and sent back to Germany, holding no further positions for the rest of the war.

Also worried was General Viktor von Schwedler, commanding officer of 4th Panzer Corps to the south of the city. His concern was rather different. He believed that using tanks in the close-quarter urban fighting in Stalingrad was a waste of his men and equipment. The infantry could, he thought, do the job just as well supported by artillery and Stukas. More importantly,

ABOVE: Hitler studies a map of Russia with (from left) Army Commander Keitel, War Minister von Brauchitsch and Paulus, October 1941.

BELOW: German artillery in Greece, April 1941. The diversion to the Balkans delayed the invasion of Russia by a month.

ABOVE: Gerd von Rundstedt (left) and Maximilian von Weichs were key players in the invasion of Russia.

BELOW: Soviet prisoners near Minsk in July 1941. Russians taken prisoner early in the war were later used as slave labour by the Germans.

ABOVE: German infantry and staff advance into Russia, August 1941. At this stage the infantry did little except try to catch up with the panzers.

ABOVE: Timoshenko commanded the Red Army when the Germans invaded.

RIGHT: A German horse-drawn supply wagon stuck at Smolensk.

ABOVE: Russian women grieve their losses, while Kiev burns behind them in a Soviet propaganda photograph from 1941.

BELOW: Civilians build anti-tank defences near Stalingrad. The vertical wall of earth was too high for German panzers to traverse.

ABOVE: Josef Stalin made himself Commissar for War, but unlike Hitler did not interfere in command decisions.

ABOVE: Soviet General Vasily Chuikov commanded the defence of Stalingrad.

ABOVE: Fedor von Bock led the 1942 campaign until sacked by Hitler.

ABOVE: Zhukov (left) planned the Soviet defence on the Volga.

ABOVE: Smoke drifts across Stalingrad as seen from the east bank of the Volga after a German bombing raid in August 1942.

RIGHT: A German aerial photograph reveals the roofless ruins of Stalingrad, autumn 1942.

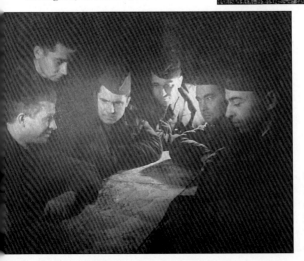

LEFT: General Aleksander Rodimtsev (left) gives orders to his 13th Guards Division in his command bunker – 95% of his men were killed.

LEFT: Sergeant Yakov Pavlov with the ruins of the building he and his men defended.

RIGHT: Soviet infantry advance down a ruined street early in the battle.

BELOW: Field Marshal Erich von Manstein (right) is widely regarded as the best strategist of the war, but he failed to rescue the 6th Army at Stalingrad.

ABOVE: General Paulus inspects Soviet positions through a periscope enlarger.

LEFT: Soviet riflemen advance behind T34 tanks. Close tank-infantry co-operation gave the Soviet forces flexibility in action.

LEFT: A Red Army man waves the Soviet flag over Stalingrad's Central Plaza after the German surrender.

RIGHT: The frozen dead of Stalingrad took months to clear away.

RIGHT: The Barmaley fountain in Stalingrad was surrounded by total devastation, but somehow survived to become a symbol of the city reborn.

Schwedler thought, was the fact that if the panzers were lost in street fighting they would be unavailable to face the next Soviet attack on the flanks. Schwedler sat down and wrote a report requesting that his tanks be taken out of the city and redeployed to the south, where the thinly-held lines faced the wide open Kalmyk Steppe.

Schwedler backed up his request by referring to a worry that had been shared by German generals in 1939 and 1940, but had since been forgotten. He pointed out that, once the armoured spearhead of a blitzkrieg attack stopped moving, the enemy might have time to think, to regroup and to attack the weakly defended corridor behind the spearhead. Like Wietersheim, Schwedler addressed his report to Paulus and again like Wietersheim he was promptly dismissed from his command.

Schwedler and Wietersheim were not the only ones to suffer. One part of the Soviet offensive had involved launching simultaneous, small-scale attacks elsewhere along the southern front. One of these struck a section of the line being held by the Italian units. Writing after the war, General Günther Blumentritt explained what had happened next. At this point Blumentritt was based at the OKH, where he was in charge of supplies and transportation on the Eastern Front. He had previously served as Chief of Staff to the 4th Army and had been a successful infantry officer. According to Blumentritt's account:

'I was sent to the Italian sector west of Stalingrad as an alarming report had come that the Russians had penetrated it and made a large breach. On arrival I found that the attack had been made by only one Russian battalion, but that an entire Italian division had fallen back. I took immediate steps to close the gap, filling it with an Alpine division and elements of the 6th German Division.

'I spent ten days in that sector and after returning made a written report to the effect that it would not be safe to hold such a long defensive flank during the winter. The railheads were as much

as 200 kilometres [124 miles] behind the front, and the bare nature of the country meant that there was little timber available for constructing defences. Such German divisions as were available were holding frontages of 50 or 60 kilometres [31 to 37 miles]. There were no proper trenches nor any fixed positions.

'General Halder read the report and agreed with it. He suggested to Hitler that the assault to capture Stalingrad should be stopped in view of the increasing resistance that it was meeting, and the increasing signs of danger to the long-stretched flank. But Hitler would not listen. Towards the end of September the tension between the Führer and Halder increased and their arguments became more bitter. To see the Führer discussing plans with Halder was an interesting experience. The Führer used to move his hands in big sweeps over the map – "Push here" he would say or "Push there". It was all vague and regardless of practical problems. There was no doubt he would have liked to remove the whole General staff if he could. He felt they were half-hearted about his ideas.

'Finally, General Halder made it clear that he refused to take the responsibility of continuing the attack with winter approaching. He was dismissed at the end of September and replaced by General [Kurt] Zeitzler.

'There would have been no problem withdrawing at this time. The German troops were now properly equipped for winter fighting and had got over their fear of the unknown that had frightened them in the previous autumn. But they were not strong enough to hold on where they were and Russian strength was growing week by week. However, Hitler would not budge. His instinct had been proved right the year before and he was sure it would be justified again. So he insisted on No Withdrawal.'

Officially Halder was not sacked, probably because he was too highly regarded by other senior officers for

Hitler to admit to an open breach with him. Instead he was moved to the 'Führer Reserve', a sort of clearing house for senior commanders awaiting a new position. The innovation allowed generals to remain on the active list – with the seniority, pay and other benefits that went with it – even though they had no actual command. Most generals passed through the Führer Reserve at one time or another, usually staying for only a few weeks. Halder never left it and was officially still there when the war ended.

Zeitzler takes over at the OKH

The man Hitler brought in to replace Halder as chief of the OKH was Kurt Zeitzler, who had previously been chief of staff to both Kleist and Rundstedt. Zeitzler was very different from Halder. He was 11 years younger and had gained direct experience in panzer units, especially when chief of staff to Kleist. While Halder was a gifted and respected strategist, Zeitzler lacked any real talent in that direction, being better at tactics. His main talent, however, was in logistics.

During the initial invasion of Russia in 1941, Kleist's panzer group had begun by heading east, and had then turned south for the Black Sea to cut off the retreat of the Soviets in the Carpathians. It had then turned back north to meet Guderian in the vast encirclement at Kiev before turning south yet again to drive down the Donets Basin and isolate the Russian forces in the Crimea. When Hitler congratulated Kleist on his successes, the panzer general was generous enough to tell him that his victories would have been impossible if Zeitzler had not arranged adequate supplies. Hitler then sent for Zeitzler. He asked the young staff officer to give a talk at the OKH on how he had done it. Hitler had remembered Zeitzler and he now appointed him over the heads of several more senior generals.

There was more to it than simply wanting a younger, more energetic man with experience of panzers in charge of the OKH. A trait of Hitler's that was coming increasingly to the fore as the war progressed was that of promoting men unexpectedly, and then using them to carry out unpleasant or controversial tasks. Hitler calculated, very often correctly, that the men would be so grateful for their unexpected promotion that they would cheerfully carry out the appointed task. If, in time, they too began to have scruples about what they were being asked to do, they could be replaced by other men, whose rapid promotion would again make them grateful to Hitler.

The task that Hitler wanted Zeitzler to do was to implement his strategy of continuing the offensive at Stalingrad into the coming winter. Hitler believed that any large-scale Soviet winter attack would fall on Army Group Centre and that he could therefore keep his forces in the south on the offensive. He also knew that many of his own generals disagreed and wanted the southern armies pulled back to a more easily defended line far to the rear of their current positions. The question was not so much if Zeitzler would do as he was told, but whether or not Hitler was right. And more crucially what was going to happen if he was wrong.

Meanwhile, the terrible fighting in Stalingrad continued.

7
THE TRACTOR FACTORY

In early October 1942, General Sir Charles Gwynn, a retired British army officer, was asked by a British magazine to write an appreciation of how the war had gone over the summer of 1942, and what he expected would happen in the course of the winter.

Stalingrad as Hitler's obsession

Gwynn was no fool. He had been commissioned into the Royal Engineers in 1889 and had fought his way across three continents before joining military intelligence. He had won a clutch of awards, including the Distinguished Service Order, and had been created a Knight Commander of the Order of the Bath on his retirement in 1931. His works on combating guerrilla warfare remained standard reading in military colleges around the world for decades and are still used today.

The article he wrote was lengthy and exhaustive, even sparing a paragraph for Madagascar, where the Free French and the British were seeking to wrest the island from the Vichy French before Pétain allowed the Japanese to build a submarine base there. The section on Stalingrad was quite long. After reviewing the situation to date, and commenting on the apparently pointless waste of men and equipment lost in the assault, Gwynn continued:

'The German must, from a purely military point of view, have begun to doubt whether it is really worth expending men and material in the attempt to complete the capture of the city by assault. He has already achieved a great part of his object, for he has practically destroyed Stalingrad as a centre of war industries, and has gained a position which enables him to interrupt through traffic on the Volga. The attainment of his full object is evidently going to be no easy matter – it would mean further loss of time and might necessitate damaging his own army more than that of the enemy.

'If he left an investing force at Stalingrad to maintain the advantage he has already secured might he not divert the bulk of his striking force to a more worthwhile object? His army pressing in the direction of the Grozny oilfield and the Caspian is held up on the Terek River. By strongly reinforcing it could he not set it again in motion? During the winter it might well be more important to hold air bases in the Caspian from which shipping, carrying

Baku oil and Allied war material from Iran, could be attacked than to be established on the banks of a frozen Volga. Since his capture of Novorossiysk, his troops there have failed to make further progress. Do they not require reinforcements in order to capture Tuapse and thereby further restrict the activities of the Russian Black Sea Fleet? Cessation of attacks on Stalingrad would in any case relieve the strain on his communications and supply routes, and allow him to give more weight to the Caucasus operations.

'But would Hitler consent to such moves? The prestige of the Reichswehr was deeply committed, and failure to take Stalingrad coming after failure to capture Leningrad and Moscow would provide fresh proof that it was not invincible.'

Gwynn was undoubtedly correct in every respect. The effort made in Stalingrad was depriving German armies elsewhere of the men and weapons that they needed to complete their tasks. The Germans would have been much better advised to halt their attacks on Stalingrad, leave a smaller force to watch the Soviets and switch reserves to other tasks. But Gwynn was also correct to point out that by this date Hitler was so obsessed by the city that he would refuse to contemplate anything that might detract from its rapid capture. Less than a week after Gwynn's article was published, the German propaganda ministry issued a statement in Berlin to the pressmen of neutral states, that was headed 'Stalingrad will be Taken'.

The bloodbath in Stalingrad would continue unabated.

At this critical juncture, Hitler had a blazing row with his Chief of Operational Staff at the OKW, General Alfred Jodl. As we shall see in Chapter 9, the dispute was prompted by events in the Caucasus, but it was to have a direct bearing on the campaign at Stalingrad. In the wake of the dispute, Hitler asked the head of the Army Personnel Office, General Rudolf Schmundt, to draw up a short list of men who had the skills and experience to replace Jodl should Hitler decide to sack him. Top of the list was that highly talented staff administration officer, but none too competent battlefield commander, General Friedrich Paulus. Schmundt was sent off to Stalingrad to talk to Paulus, to see if he would be interested.

Schmundt arrived at a crucial time. The first attack into the city had been brought to a halt and Paulus was laying his plans for a second assault, one that he hoped would be final. Schmundt arrived and announced that he had good news for Paulus from Hitler. Paulus assumed that he meant that the reinforcements that he had requested so often were finally on their way. He launched into a long tirade about the lack of equipment, the tiredness of his men and the poor supplies, before concluding that he had achieved all of his original objectives but was now being asked to capture Stalingrad as well. When he had finished, Schmundt brushed his comments aside and then gave him the news of a possible move to replace Jodl. Paulus made some modest, self-deprecating remarks about how his talents were not really up to the senior task, but made it very clear that he would accept immediately if Jodl were to be dismissed.

When Schmundt left to return to Hitler at Werewolf, Paulus at once ordered his staff to hurry forward the plans for the renewed assault. This time it was to be the northern part of Stalingrad that would be the focus for the assault. The key targets for the offensive were to be three large, stoutly-built structures that dominated the surrounding townscape.

They stood in a line a few hundred feet from the west bank of the Volga. If they could be captured, German guns would be able to sweep the Volga and the city centre. The three buildings were the Dzerzhinsky Tractor Factory, the Barrikady Gun Factory and the Red October Steel Factory.

At about this time the Soviet poet Konstantin Simonov was sent to Stalingrad to write a series of articles for the Soviet press. In his first articles he described his arrival:

'I crossed the Volga to Stalingrad. The battlefield stretched ahead in the brief southern dusk – smoking mounds, burning streets. The enemy's white signal flares shot into the sky.

'Seated beside me on the ferry was a 20-year-old Ukrainian girl, a doctor's assistant. It was her fifth trip to the city, helping to evacuate the wounded. Nurses and doctors' assistants work in the very front line. They arrange for the wounded to be carried to the far end of the city, to the quayside, where there is a shuttle service of ferries and other boats which convey the wounded in the opposite direction.

'"I should be accustomed to it, I suppose," the girl suddenly said to me as we approached the Stalingrad bank. "Yet every time I come I am afraid to land. I've been wounded twice, once seriously, but I never once thought I would die because I have seen so little of life yet."

'Her wide-open eyes were sad. I guessed what she must feel to be 20 years old and twice wounded,

to have been at war for fifteen months and to be making her fifth trip to Stalingrad. In a quarter of an hour she would be threading her way through blazing houses, forcing a passage through side streets blocked with debris, heedless of shell fragments, seeking the wounded and carrying them away.'

German tactics

To help his men prepare for the renewed assault, Paulus had devised new tactics and brought up a devastating new weapon: Dora. The innocuously named Dora was, in fact, one of the most powerful and lethal siege cannons ever built. It was the largest calibre (80 cm; 31 inches) rifled weapon in the history of artillery and its 7 tonne shells were the heaviest ever fired. It was so large that it could be fired only from a special carriage that was mounted on twin railway lines running side by side. The entire weapon weighed 1,350 tonnes, was 47 metres (155 feet) long and 7.1 metres (23 feet) wide. It could fire shells with accuracy to a range of 38 kilometres (23 miles), though it could fire only 14 times a day. It was aimed at command posts, concrete emplacements and other targets the more mobile artillery could not tackle.

To aid the street clearing that would be needed, Paulus had been given a number of specialist engineering units. These included building demolition teams and miners. The infantry had also been retrained and reformed to mimic the successful stormtrooper tactics that had been used to smash through the trenches of the Allies during the German offensive of March 1918. Groups of a dozen men were equipped with submachine guns and ample supplies of grenades, while one man had a heavy machine-gun and another a flame-thrower. These stormtroopers would charge forward to lead an assault. Their task was to punch through the Soviet front line at weak places, while leaving strongpoints untouched. They would then set up a new front line across which the Soviets could not move supplies or reinforcements. Behind this new front line the rest of the German infantry and tanks would then eliminate the isolated strongpoints.

Stukas would be used to destroy any strongpoint that looked to be too tough for the ground forces to tackle. Other bombers would pound the rear areas behind the Soviet front lines to disrupt the flow of supplies and reinforcements.

Soviet tactics

The Soviets too had devised new tactics. Orders sent out from Chuikov's new headquarters, a cave hollowed out of the cliffs dropping down to the Volga, told infantry officers how to mount an attack on German positions.

'Get close to the enemy. Move on all fours, making use of craters and ruins. Dig your trenches by night and camouflage them by day. Make your build-up for the attack stealthily and without any noise. Surprise must be on your side.

'Each man must have a tommy-gun and twelve grenades. Two of you get into the house together.

You and a grenadier, both be lightly dressed. You without your knapsack and the grenadier bare of equipment. Send the grenadier in first, then you after. Go through the whole house, again always the grenadier first into every room and you after. There is one strict rule – give yourself elbow room. At every step danger lurks. Don't worry, a grenade goes into every room first, then follow with the gun. A grenade, then you. Again and again. A room? A grenade! A bend in a corridor? A grenade! And always keep moving.

'Remember that fighting inside a building is always frantic. So always be prepared for the unexpected. Keep a sharp look out. The enemy may try a counterattack. Don't be afraid. You have the initiative. Act more ruthlessly with your grenade, your gun, your knife, your spade.'

Snipers were also being deployed in increasingly large numbers. It had long been a practice in the Red Army for the best shot in a unit to be designated a sniper. His task was to hide up somewhere and try to shoot enemy officers. The more successful snipers were given special sniper rifles fitted with telescopic sights.

On 22 September the 1047th Rifle Regiment had arrived in Stalingrad and with it the regimental sniper, Sergeant Major Vasily Zaytsev. Zaytsev was a crack shot, but his real skills lay in being able to conceal himself perfectly while still allowing a clear field of view across enemy lines. He was skilled at hiding at night beneath piles of bricks, in drains, behind refuse or in all sorts of unlikely places. He then lay absolutely still throughout the day, sometimes for days on end until a target showed itself, when he would shoot just once. A second shot would attract German attention, so having killed a victim Zaytsev would then lie completely still until darkness allowed him to move. He worked in a team with an assistant named Nikolay Kulikov, who would lie in hiding within shouting range and act as a scout for Zaytsev, keeping an eye open for things the sniper could not see.

VASILY ZAYTSEV

On 31 January 2006, Russian sniper Vasily Zaytsev was buried beside the huge war memorial in the centre of Volgograd (formerly Stalingrad). As might be expected for a highly decorated Russian soldier, the Russian military were out in force for the occasion. Rather more surprisingly, the American military were also there in full dress to lay a wreath on the grave. The reason that Zaytsev was so highly regarded in both life and death was not so much due to his war record – spectacular though that was – but to his skills as a teacher.

Zaytsev was born in 1915 and grew up in a rural area of the Urals with his grandfather, who earned a living as a hunter. Zaytsev later claimed to have shot his first wolf when he was just five years old, and certainly by his teens he was an accomplished deer hunter. He later joined the Soviet Navy and when World War II broke out was working as a clerk in the Pacific port of

Vladivostock. Seeking action he transferred to the 1047th Rifle Regiment and soon earned a reputation for accurate shooting.

In September 1942 the 1047th Rifle Regiment was sent to fight in Stalingrad, then under siege by the German 6th Army. He was in action one day when his commanding officer pointed out a German officer about 800 metres away and asked Zaytsev if he could hit the enemy. Zaytsev took careful aim with his standard-issue Mosin-Nagant rifle and shot the officer. Seconds later a German soldier came to tend the officer, Zaytsev whipped the rifle back to his shoulder and shot the second German dead as well. For this feat he was given a specially adapted sniper's Mosin with a telescopic sight.

Over the days that followed Zaytsev's score of dead Germans grew steadily. Exactly how many men he shot is unclear. Soviet propaganda almost certainly exaggerated his skills, and the often repeated boast that he averaged six dead Germans a day in October 1942 need not be treated too seriously. He was, however, clearly a highly successful sniper and good organizer. Much of his combat success was due to his partnership with Nikolay Kulikov, who spotted targets for Zaytsev. In late October, the two men were pulled out of the front line by General Chuikov, commander of the Soviet 62nd Army in Stalingrad, and ordered to teach other snipers their tactics.

It was in the Lazur Chemical Works that Zaytsev established what was to become the Sniper School where hundreds of Soviet snipers were to be trained. The men taught by Zaytsev called themselves 'Little Hares' – a play on words for the Russian for a hare *zayats* sounds similar to Zaytsev. The men were taught that it was best for snipers to work in pairs, with an observer working with the gunman. The men were to take up positions so that between them they had a wide field of view across the battlefield. Zaytsev laid great stress on camouflage, insisting that snipers should take up position at night then lie absolutely still during the day until a target presented itself. The sniper, he said, should fire only once, for a second shot would give his position away. Only after lying still for a long time should the sniper move off to find another hiding place.

Zaytsev and Kulikov were later allowed to return to the front line and fought throughout the rest of the war. Zaytsev ended the war with 224 confirmed kills, though Soviet sources have made claims that he shot more than 600 Germans, Romanians and Italians in his career. After the war he took up a career as a textile engineer and died in 1991. His funeral was quiet, but his body was later moved to be reburied with full military honours in Stalingrad, by then renamed Volgograd.

The sniper tactics developed and taught by Zaytsev remain in use today. The Russians used them in Chechnya in 1999 and the Americans put them into practice in Iraq in 2011.

*Zaytsev was played by actor Jude Law in the film **Enemy at the Gates** (2001) directed by Jean-Jacques Annaud*

Chuikov also issued the advice that was to become known as 'hugging the enemy'. The Soviets had noticed that the safest place to be was very often close to the German infantry. The Stuka pilots and the artillery gunners would avoid attacking places too close to their own men for fear of inflicting casualties.

They preferred to go after targets at least 46 metres (50 yards) from their comrades. So Chuikov gave orders that his infantry should always try to be within 46 metres (50 yards) of a German. This often led to enemies being able to hear each other breathe, talk or walk without knowing exactly where their opposite numbers were. The terrible fighting in Stalingrad was getting more deadly and ruthless by the day.

The offensive begins

At 6 am on 27 September the German offensive began. On the left was the 389th Infantry Division, which had been given the task of gaining the suburb of Orlovka, then the Barrikady. To the right the 24th Panzer Division aimed to capture a small airfield, then push on into the city centre. Further to the right again, the 100th Jäger Division (an Austrian unit) was to take over the workers' housing estate linked to the Red October Factory.

The assault was preceded by a heavy artillery and Stuka bombardment, which pounded Soviet positions in the front line and the defences behind. As the 389th Division launched its attack on the workers' houses the soldiers were surprised to see several hundred women and children break cover and run toward the Russian lines. Presumably they had been sheltering in cellars. They did not get far. The Soviet machine guns firing at the advancing Germans killed most of them in minutes. Those Germans who saw the incident were appalled. By dusk the

Germans had made advances in all areas, but progress was slow.

At dawn next day the *Luftwaffe* came down in large numbers to attack the shipping on the Volga. Civilians were still trying to get out of the city. One Soviet boatmen recorded the scene:

'By the shore were people, including many children. Using small spades, as well as their hands, they dug holes to hide from bullets and artillery shells. At dawn German planes appeared over the Volga. On a hedge-hopping flight they flew over a ferry and bombed and opened fire from machine-guns. From above, it was very well visible to the pilots, that civilians were waiting on the shore. Many times we saw enemy pilots acting as professional assassins. They opened fire on the unarmed women and children and selected targets so as to maximize the number of people killed. The pilots dropped bombs in a crowd at the moment they were beginning to board a boat,

fired at the decks of the boats, and bombed islands on which hundreds of wounded had accumulated. The people crossed the river not only on boats and barges. They sailed on overcrowded boats, even on logs, barrels, and boards bound with wire. And the Fascists opened fire from the air on each floating target. They were massacring people.'

The attack was brutal, but it succeeded in sinking five of the six large ferries. The Soviets were now reduced to using fishing smacks and rowing boats to ferry men and supplies over the Volga.

Meanwhile, Paulus had sent the 60th Motorized Infantry Division to support the 389th in its attack on Orlovka. The fresh troops went into action on 29 September and their presence was at once felt. Most of the suburb was captured, but it would take another nine days before the process was completed. In the centre of the city the Mamayev Kurgan hill was once again captured by the Germans, but then lost again.

Zhukov decided that Stalingrad was in danger

and made efforts to relieve the pressure. With cold-blooded calculation, he did the minimum possible to avoid outright disaster and kept most of his growing reserves well to the rear, out of sight of the Germans. The 39th Guards Rifle Division was sent across the river to Stalingrad, along with a couple of regiments from the 308th Rifle Division, but that was all. To the north at Rynok an offensive was launched on 30 September, but again the 16th Panzers swatted it aside without undue difficulty.

Pavlov's House

Also on 30 September the fighting began around an anonymous-looking block of flats that was to achieve fame as 'Pavlov's House'. The block of flats had been identified by Chuikov's staff to be one of the strongpoints that would hold up the German advance. The importance of the four-storey structure came from the fact that it stood on the corner of the large, open 9th January Square from which straight roads ran north and south for 914 metres (1,000 yards), while a further road ran due east to the Volga and a fourth ran due west for some 550 metres (600 yards).

A platoon of the 13th Guards commanded by Lieutenant Ivan F. Afanasiev had been sent to defend the building and had spent several days fortifying it. Afanasiev ordered all roads leading to the square, and the square itself, to be liberally strewn with mines and booby traps as well as dense thickets of barbed wire. Lightweight anti-tank rifles were installed in sandbagged emplacements on the roof while more than two dozen machine-guns were mounted in carefully concealed nests, to fire across the square and along the streets. Inside the building holes were knocked in walls to allow rapid movement between what had been separate flats. Finally a network of trenches was constructed, running back from the house towards the rear areas, along which supplies could be brought.

On the first day of fighting Afanasiev was wounded and later evacuated. That left the 45 men holding the building under the command of Senior Sergeant Yakov Pavlov, hence the building's nickname. When the German offensive reached Pavlov's House the stormtroopers tried to move around it, but found their paths blocked, or swept by gunfire from the house. A direct assault on Pavlov's House failed, as did a second and a third. Pavlov's unit commander fed men and supplies up through the trench system into the house each night, but never attempted to remove the men once they were there. At no time were there more than 50 living men in the building, though many times that number were killed there.

When the Germans eventually withdrew from 9th January Square and Pavlov's House, only Pavlov and three others of the original squad, plus two women residents, were left alive.

Many legends grew up in the Red Army about Pavlov's House. One said that Pavlov had personally destroyed 12 panzers by shooting them with an anti-tank rifle from the roof. Another had it that at night the defenders had to creep out into 9th January

Square to kick over the piles of German dead, so that they would not be used as cover for a subsequent attack. What is known for certain is that Chuikov often joked that Hitler had lost more men attacking Pavlov's House than he had done attacking Paris.

Elsewhere the fighting was just as savage, though often more fluid, with buildings changing hands several times. The closeness of the two fighting forces is shown by one of the reports sent back from Stalingrad by the poet Simonov.

'Today I spent the day at a battalion command post in the north of the city. I was accompanied by an officer from Chuikov's headquarters who knew the way. We went there last night under cover of darkness. The command post is situated in a ruined factory. The street leading north toward the German lines is under constant mortar fire. It is a dangerous place.

'The day broke and the sky paled to blue. We made our way up to an observation point overlooking *a key sector. "Make yourself comfortable, here is a well-sprung arm chair," said the man on duty. This place used to be a well-furnished fifth floor flat. Now it is open to the sky with no roof and a ruined wall. We can see German tanks moving past at the end of the street. A German motorcyclist races past. Then infantrymen come into view, and a mine in the street goes off. My companion said we needed to leave the post and return to the battalion command post. I stayed there while messengers came and went giving news of the German attack made down the street, but it was driven off.'*

On 1 October men of the German 295th Division found a drain that led around the right flank of the Soviet 13th Guards positions. They clambered through the drain in strength that night and at dawn they emerged to attack the rear of the 13th Guards. The attack reached the Volga, but by throwing all of his reserves into the combat, Rodimtsev pushed the

Germans back from the river and secured his right flank.

The next day a German shell hit an oil storage tank close to Chuikov's cave headquarters. The oil caught fire, flooded out of the tank and cascaded through the streets to pour over the cliff top and into the Volga. The burning torrent swept over the mouth of the cave and destroyed all of the radio aerials that Chuikov was using to keep in touch with his units and with Zhukov. The Soviets in Stalingrad were leaderless. On the far bank of the Volga men watched the waterfall of fire, assumed that Chuikov and his headquarters had been destroyed and alerted Zhukov's headquarters to the disaster.

Zhukov ordered his radio signaller to keep up a constant stream of signals to try to raise Chuikov. Eventually a faint signal was received in reply. 'Where are you?' asked Zhukov, thinking that Chuikov had not been in his headquarters when disaster struck but was elsewhere in Stalingrad.

'Well,' came Chuikov's reply. 'You see all those

flames?' The burning oil had swept right past the cave and miraculously nobody had been hurt.

Lessons from Verdun

On the German side, comparisons with the great First World War battle of Verdun were becoming increasingly common. That battle, fought in 1916, had left a savage scar on the collective memory of the German army. The German commander in 1916, Erich von Falkenhayn, had concluded that the trench systems on the Western Front were so strong that the Germans could not achieve a breakthrough.

Instead he sought to destroy the French army in a massive battle of attrition. He chose Verdun because the town marked a salient (bulge in the line), which protruded into German territory, so German artillery could be installed on three sides of the French. In addition, rail lines ran close to the German lines, ensuring a plentiful flow of supplies and ammunition for the offensive. Falkenhayn also knew that Verdun had never fallen to an enemy assault – not even to

Attila the Hun. The French would be willing to make any sacrifice to hold on to Verdun, and Falkenhayn aimed to make that price very high indeed.

His initial plan was to subject Verdun to a massive artillery barrage, followed by light infantry assaults that would make the French believe that an attack was imminent. They would then feed more troops into position, who would be killed by renewed German artillery fire. The campaign opened in February and went exactly to plan, until the Kaiser got carried away by the reports and insisted on full infantry attacks, which saw German casualties rise.

For months the fighting continued, with the French taking the heaviest casualties. Eventually Falkenhayn called off the battle, since his own men had been killed in large numbers and the French showed no signs of collapsing. Not until after the war did the Germans learn that the French army had been on the brink of disaster. Entire divisions had mutinied, gone on the rampage and refused to march to Verdun. Another week or two of effort and Germany might have won the war.

The Germans took two lessons from Verdun. The first was that battles of prestige could be horribly costly for little gain. The second was that in a war of attrition the side that was able to put in the final reserves was going to win. If Stalingrad was to be a second Verdun, two questions needed answering: which side was losing men fastest and which side would be able to put in the last reserves? For the men on the ground it was the bleak prospect of facing a gruesome death in a grinding battle of attrition that dominated all.

Barrikady Factory

The Barrikady Factory was defended by the 308th Rifle Division. The men had been recruited from Siberia and even in the Red Army had a reputation for toughness and ruthlessness. Their commander, Colonel Leonid Gurtiev, was even tougher. When training his men to dig trenches he would wait until they were finished, then get a T34 tank to drive over the excavations, with the men cowering at the bottom. And that was just the training.

The assault on the Barrikady Factory was preceded by Stuka and high-level bombing raids that lasted all day. Next morning the Stukas came again, followed by artillery shells. As soon as the shelling stopped the panzers rumbled forward, accompanied by infantry. The Siberians leapt from their trenches to attack, only to be met by a murderous hail of fire that cut them down in large numbers. The move had, however, served to bring the panzers to a halt, where they were soon assailed by anti-tank fire from the Siberian 96 mm guns hidden in the rubble. The panzers drew back and the Stukas came again. That night the Siberians crept forward with anti-tank mines, to strew the area cleared by the Germans. T34 tanks came up to join the Siberians in their limited counterattacks and to be hidden in the ruins to act as anti-tank guns.

A Soviet Army report recounts one incident from Paulus's northern offensive. The report was written by the commander of an anti-aircraft battery located on the Penkovatyj Island in the Volga.

'Report from the commander of the A.A. Battery, 1051 Rifle Regiment, 300 Inf. Div.

'At dawn on October 20 1942, the observation post reported: in mist in the Tomilino area, the rumble of ship motors is audible. Approaching the island are 2 storm-boats and 12 rowboats, transporting approximately a battalion of German commandos. The A.A. battery gunners raised an alarm. When the enemy boats were 150 meters [500 feet] away, the battery began a destructive fire. The rifle and machine gun companies of 1 Battalion, 1049 Rifle Regiment also began firing. The German artillery began a strong counter fire. Enemy machine-guns fired on our defences from the right bank and from the boats. The battery's guns have destroyed the German storm-boats, and double M.G. with the help of the riflemen have destroyed the rowboats. The Germans commandos are completely destroyed in the water. No German soldiers set foot on the island. Battle casualties: 1 killed, 6 wounded.

'These soldiers showed particular courage:

*1. Sergeant Kuzmenko – A.A. gun
   commander.*
*2. Junior Sergeant Temirgalyjev –
   gunlayer.*

*Signature: **Junior Lieutenant I. Chenin.'***

Paulus saw his attack grinding forward with steady but slow progress. He summoned in the 94th Infantry Division and the 14th Panzer Division to join the assault. Perhaps belatedly, Paulus realized that Soviet heavy artillery on the east bank of the Volga was causing his men difficulties in getting supplies up to the front line, and was taking a heavy toll on his fighting men. Unlike the German gunners, the Soviet artillerymen had no scruples about shelling the front lines even if that meant inflicting death on their own men.

On 5 October Chuikov received a visitor who

was not terribly welcome. General Filipp Golikov was Yeremenko's chief of intelligence and deputy commander. He came across the Volga under fire to deliver to Chuikov in person a message direct from Stalin and to emphasize its importance. Stalin's message began by praising Chuikov and his men for their determination and fighting abilities. Then came the sting. Stalin ordered Chuikov to retake those parts of the city centre that were in the hands of the Germans. Chuikov knew that he would be lucky to hold what he had without reinforcements and that driving the Germans out was impossible. He held his tongue. Arguing with Stalin was never a good idea.

Tractor Factory

Two days after Golikov's short visit, the 14th Panzer Division launched a major effort to take the Tractor Factory, with 60th Motorized Division in support. On the southern edge of the assault the Germans achieved a limited breakthrough and headed for an underground workshop where local men were repairing and maintaining T34 tanks. The poet Simonov recorded what happened next:

'The workers heard that the German tanks had broken through the defences and were making straight for their factory. The directors and the repair shop superintendent called a workers' meeting. A number of tank crews were selected. Then repairs were speeded up on a few tanks that were nearing completion. When the job was finished the workers jumped into the tanks and set off to meet the enemy, followed by detachments of their comrades with rifles and grenades. They met the Germans at a stone bridge across a narrow ravine. The tanks confronted each other across the bridge and a furious gun duel ensued. Meanwhile, German machine-gunners began to clamber down the bank in an attempt to reach the other side. The factory workers engaged them. Barricades were built in all the streets leading to the bridge. As during the Civil War, the wives *carried ammunition to their husbands. Young girls moved about the advanced positions, bandaging the wounded and dragging them to safety. Many died, but the workers held the Germans until Red Army reinforcements arrived to plug the gap.*

'I stood on this bridge and gazed along the ravine. It was an extraordinary sight. The steep banks hummed like an ant heap. They were honeycombed with caves. The entrances were covered with boards, rags, anything the women of Stalingrad could lay hands on to protect their families from the rain and wind. The sight filled me with bitterness.'

Though the Germans failed to take the entire Tractor Factory they did make significant advances. They were now in a position to sweep the whole Volga with machine-guns or artillery. Crossing the river was becoming increasingly hazardous. The crews of all of the remaining craft, and those of barges brought downstream at night, were forced to join the

NKVD and were formed into the 71st Special Service Company. This was no favour. Discipline in the NKVD was even more ferocious and deadly than in the Red Army. Moreover it gave the Communist Party control over movements across the Volga, not the Army, for the 71st Special Service Company came under the orders of the NKVD on the east bank, which had not come under the command of Chuikov.

It was a sign that the crisis of the campaign was approaching.

8
STALEMATE

If Chuikov was receiving impossible orders from Stalin, the orders Paulus was getting from Hitler were just as impracticable. On 8 October Paulus reported that his latest offensive had come to a halt. The Soviet hold on the west bank was tenuous to say the least. The Soviets were divided into a number of pockets strung out along the Volga, each receiving limited supplies from across the river. Yet Paulus was unable to destroy the final enclaves of Soviet resistance.

Hitler orders a new offensive

Hitler's response came almost by return. Another major offensive had to be mounted. He set 14 October as the date for the new attack. Hitler has often been condemned for this order, and for several other mistakes made during this disastrous campaign, but here at least he was not entirely to blame. The reports on which he had based his decision were seriously inaccurate. As we have seen, German intelligence had overestimated the number of Soviet forces on the central section of the line to the north of Stalingrad, which meant that they believed that the Russians had fewer forces available for Stalingrad than was the case. The mistake was compounded by reports generated by Paulus and the 6th Army. These overestimated the casualties that they had been inflicting on the Russians in Stalingrad. Overestimating enemy losses is a not unusual military fault, but Paulus's figures had been confirmed by Weichs, who should have been monitoring and checking them instead of merely passing them on.

The result was that the Germans thought they had destroyed a larger proportion of the Soviet forces than was the case. Hitler imagined that his position in Stalingrad in October 1942 was similar to that of Falkenhayn at Verdun in September 1916. He was convinced that the enemy forces were on the brink of total collapse and that one last kick would see them destroyed. Hitler did not want to repeat Falkenhayn's mistake of calling off an attack just as it was about to succeed. Instead he made a different mistake – renewing an attack when it had no chance of success.

Paulus decided that his new assault would be directed at the same northern sector as his previous offensive. This time the attack would be delivered on a narrower front so that a greater concentration of force could be brought into play. The Tractor Factory was the first target, and once that was captured the assault was to push on to the banks of the Volga.

At 6 am on 14 October the attack was opened by a great formation of Stuka dive bombers, that came down to pound the area in front of the 14th

Panzer Division. This was followed up by artillery fire, mortars and assault guns. General Viktor Zholudev, commander of the 37th Guards Division, was buried in his command bunker by German shells and had to wait for several disconcerting hours until his men managed to dig him out.

Then the panzers and the infantry moved forward into the wasteland left by the bombers and the artillery. By now it came as no surprise to the Germans to learn that Russian soldiers had not only survived the barrage, but were in place and ready to fight. As planned, the German stormtroopers surged forward through weaker sections of the Soviet line to isolate strongpoints. In several places, the surrounded Soviets chose to launch suicidal but deeply unnerving attacks on the Germans rather than remain on the defensive.

On the second day of the offensive an infantry unit of the 14th Panzer Division broke through the Soviet lines and reached the Volga. The Germans fanned out along the banks, and in the afternoon found themselves in possession of the cave where Chuikov had made his headquarters. The Soviet commander was gone, however, having hurriedly moved south out of harm's way. Nevertheless, his army was very far from being out of danger. That evening the medical services reported that 3,500 badly wounded men had been treated at military hospitals. Nobody knew how many men were dead.

The following day the Germans began an advance along the river bank, with the objective of cutting off the surviving Russians from their sources of supply across the Volga. Another attack was launched from the now secure Tractor Factory, towards the Barrikady Factory. A force of Soviet tanks stopped the latter attack, though at very heavy cost, but the advance down the river bank seemed unstoppable. The 112th Division and the 115th Division were in the rubble around the Tractor Factory, cut off from Chuikov.

No aid for Chuikov

Chuikov sent a radio message to Yeremenko and Khrushchev, in which he requested permission to move the bulk of his administration staff to the east bank of the Volga, while he and his key command personnel remained on the west bank. Khrushchev feared Stalin's reaction to this request and did not even pass it on. He told Chuikov that his clerks would have to stay put. Later that day, the administration staff were issued with rifles and grenades. By dusk some of them had gone into action.

Yeremenko himself crossed the Volga under cover of night to see what was going on. He found Chuikov grimly determined to hold on until death, but he was very tired, dirty and short of virtually anything useful. Zholudev was at Chuikov's command bunker when Yeremenko arrived, so Yeremenko asked him how his 37th Guards were faring. Zholudev burst into tears and collapsed, unable to answer.

Next day the commanders of the isolated 112th and 115th Divisions got through to Chuikov on the radio to report that their units had been effectively destroyed. They asked permission to evacuate the survivors across the Volga, but Chuikov refused.

When he later discovered that the two divisions were, in fact, still fighting at this point he had the commanding officers court-martialled and shot.

Meanwhile, Chuikov was on the move again. On 17 October he moved his headquarters to a bunker near Mamayev Kurgan, still further south. He radioed Yeremenko to ask if the heavy artillery on the east bank could open fire on those areas where the Germans were massing for a renewed assault. Yeremenko refused, stating that there was no ammunition available. The German advance continued. By 25 October Chuikov commanded about a dozen separate pockets of territory, each held by a mix of fragmented units. Supplies were brought across the Volga by rowing boat, then carried up the steep banks to reach the different enclaves. The German advance had been relentless, though achieved at very heavy cost. Chuikov can have been under no illusion as to his eventual fate. He had no way of knowing why Yeremenko had told him that the artillery had no ammunition, but he must have guessed that it could have been put to better use elsewhere. Perhaps the Soviet high command had abandoned hope of holding on to Stalingrad.

The Germans dig in

On 1 November the Germans launched a new attack, this time on the Red October Factory. Again Chuikov radioed for heavy artillery support. This time he got it and the German attack ended with the attackers going to ground. Chuikov was told that he could expect no further help of this kind. What he did not realize was that he could also expect no further major German offensives.

All across the Eastern Front the cold weather was drawing in as the days got shorter and winter approached. This was to be the Germans' second winter in Russia. Although they were now much better prepared to endure the biting cold and howling blizzards, they were very far from being equipped for winter campaigning. It was impossible for the Germans to undertake any major operations with confidence, so all commanders, from field marshals down to lieutenants, were turning their minds to defensive measures that would allow them to survive the winter without losing too many men or too much territory. Trenches and tank traps were being hurriedly dug before the ground froze solid, while trees were felled and their timbers incorporated into dugouts, huts and storage depots. Although Hitler was known to be firmly opposed to any withdrawals, some surreptitious frontline changes were undertaken, enabling the Germans to move back to hills, rivers and other lines that could be more easily defended. Every German officer remembered the Soviet attacks around Moscow the previous winter, and had no wish to be caught unawares.

In Stalingrad the October digging-in was conducted as efficiently as elsewhere. In rear areas field hospitals were constructed, along with command posts and supply dumps. Often these were built underground or camouflaged among the ruins of the suburbs. More than one general had his headquarters built into a network of interconnecting cellars beneath ruined houses that were left unrepaired, so that nothing was visible from the air. Many of the ruins were plundered for timber, tiles, bricks and other building materials. Lorry after lorry loaded up with such spoils and carried them out to units camping on the open steppes. Nobody wanted to be exposed to the cold and the snow when they could have warm, brick-lined dugouts or timber huts.

The men in the front line in Stalingrad began converting their positions into defensive bastions. Houses were converted into machine-gun nests and sniper hideouts. Windows were covered with wire mesh to stop Soviet grenades from coming in unexpectedly, sewers were blocked to stop surprise Russian attacks and barbed wire was liberally strung about to slow down any Russian advances. Mines were put on all roads and booby traps were inserted into houses, to force the Soviets to advance warily, and therefore slowly. All personnel who would not be needed for the winter were sent hundreds of miles to the rear, so that the overworked supply lines would not have to carry their food all the way to Stalingrad.

Not that anyone expected to take things easy. Orders from the OKH, signed by Hitler, called for an 'active defence'. This meant that aggressive patrolling would be carried out regularly, that small offensives would be launched locally whenever there was a good chance of success, and that the artillery would keep up sporadic fire on Soviet supply lines.

From what the Germans could make out, the Soviets were likewise digging in for the winter. They too were digging trenches, felling trees and improving the defensive positioning of their front lines. In places the front lines edged further and further apart, as both sides moved away from holding vulnerable territory. There was only one section of the front where the Russians were not obviously going on to the defensive: Rzhev. This town lay in the region where the German Army Group Centre held the line, and was near the northern edge of where German intelligence believed the main Russian strength to lie. Around Rzhev the Soviets were mounting a large number of small-scale attacks on the Germans, as if probing the German positions to discover their layout and strength. The moves convinced the senior planners at the OKH that it was here that the Russians would launch their winter campaign, expected in later November or early December.

Hitler agreed, for the most part, and German plans were laid accordingly. However, according to General Walter Warlimont, then serving at the OKW, one strategic conference was interrupted by Hitler, who in an uncharacteristically pensive mood pointed to the Don River west of Stalingrad. He then regaled his staff with the tale of how the Soviet Red Army had won a battle there against the Tsarist White Army in 1919. Hitler was referring to what is known as the Battle of Tsaritsyn, the former name of Stalingrad. The Whites had defeated the Reds on the open steppe and pushed them back into Tsaritsyn, which was then put under siege. The White forces appeared to be on the brink of victory when Red Army reinforcements arrived unexpectedly and launched a savage assault west of the city, which drove the Whites back in confusion.

The Red Army Commissar who had authorized the offensive, against orders from Lenin in Moscow, had been a youthful Stalin.

'I wonder if he would try the same thing again,' mused Hitler. He asked for a report on the state of the Romanian forces that were holding the lines west and south of the German 6th Army in Stalingrad.

Romanian woes

When that report arrived it made for woeful reading. The Romanian army had gone to war expecting to carry out secondary operations, such as capturing Russian positions cut off by the panzer blitzkrieg. It was neither equipped nor trained for frontline modern fighting. Having last undergone a major reform at the end of the First World War, it largely reflected the conventional thinking that had then been prevalent. The bulk of the army was made up of infantry divisions, trained in trench fighting and open skirmishing. The equipment of the infantry was out of date. Their main anti-tank gun was the French Canon 37 mm mle.1916, a First World War vintage weapon that the Germans had captured in 1940 and handed over to their allies. There were several cavalry brigades, which had been effective in scouting and patrolling over the summer of 1942. The Romanians had very little in the way of tanks and what they had was outdated.

The report was given to Hitler, but whether he read it or not is unknown. He certainly never referred to it again, or to the 1919 Battle of Tsaritsyn.

But if Hitler chose to ignore the Romanians, their own commander was starting to get anxious. General Petre Dumitrescu had fought through the First World War, rising to be a colonel by 1919, and in the 1930s had been attached to the French army for a while. He had seen the state of the French army before its catastrophic defeat in 1940 and was painfully aware that his own forces were very similar. He made repeated demands to be given up-to-date German anti-tank guns, but it was not until October that he was given a paltry six 75 mm guns for each of his divisions, and they came with minimal stocks of ammunition.

Realizing that he was not going to get any more equipment before the spring of 1943, and possibly not even then, Dumitrescu decided to make one last effort to get the Germans to understand the critical condition of his forces. He had his staff draw up a detailed report analyzing his defensive positions, the equipment of his men and the strength and positions of the Russian troops facing his own. Dumitrescu sent it to Weichs at the headquarters of Army Group B on 29 October. The report not only gave a clear analysis of the Romanian forces, but its estimate of the Russian strength was far in excess of that held by the OKW, and so by Weichs. The report also detailed the movement of reserves up to the Russian front line, the number of small probing attacks made by Soviet infantry over the previous month and a couple of statements from Russian prisoners, who claimed that a major offensive was being prepared. Dumitrescu's report concluded that the Soviets were about to attack the Romanian section of the line in great strength, and it estimated that the blow would fall within four weeks.

Weichs was understandably alarmed. He ordered Richthofen to fly a series of reconnaissance flights over the Russian front and rear areas facing the Romanians, and Paulus was summoned back to the Army Group HQ at Starobelsk to discuss both Dumitrescu's report and Richthofen's findings. The meeting concluded that the Russians had concentrated four divisions (three infantry and one armoured) at Kletskaya and three divisions (two infantry and one armoured) at Blynov. Their combined strength was no greater than that which the Russians had used at Rynok some weeks earlier, an attack that had been beaten off with very little trouble. Paulus and Weichs concluded that the Russians were intending to attack the Romanians, but that the German reserves would be equal to the task. They believed that the initial attacks, wherever they were made, would punch through the Romanian front lines. Once the positions of the Russian attacks were known, however, German forces would rush to contain them, and then deploy to push them back over the Don. Nobody in Army Group B was unduly worried – apart from Dumitrescu.

Dumitrescu contacted Marshal Antonescu back in Bucharest and explained the situation in no uncertain terms. Antonescu contacted Hitler, but was fobbed off. The Romanian tried again, and was rewarded with promises of a personal meeting with the Führer to discuss the Romanian contribution to the war in Russia. As events would prove, the meeting would come too late.

A final attempt before winter

One other man was getting concerned by how events were taking shape. Kurt Zeitzler, Hitler's new Chief of the Army Staff, had come from a logistics background and had a keen understanding of the supply problems his armies would be facing over the coming winter. He also understood that the Russian supply system in the area had depended on river traffic along the Volga. Most of those ferries had now been sunk and the Volga was freezing. 'If we cannot clear up the situation [in Stalingrad] now, when the Russians are in difficulties and the Volga is blocked with ice floes, then we shall never be able to do so,' he wrote.

Zeitzler and Hitler told Paulus he had to make one more attempt at capturing Stalingrad before a halt was called for the winter. Paulus was given four new pioneer battalions, trained especially in subterranean fighting in sewers, cellars and caves. The surviving men of the 71st, 79th, 100th, 295th, 305th and 389th divisions were reorganized into stormtrooper and follow-up units.

At dawn on 11 November, Richthofen's Stukas and other bombers once again pounded the Russian front lines, concentrating on the area north of Mamayev Kurgan. Then the German tanks and infantry moved forward, aided by the pioneers – who crawled through the sewers to emerge on the flanks and the rear of the Russian defensive positions. For two days the German attack went as well as might be expected. Several Russian positions were overrun, others were surrounded and in half a dozen places the Germans reached the Volga. Chuikov's positions were further broken up and fragmented.

Then the Russian defence became firmer. The Germans were exhausted, but hand-outs of amphetamine drugs gave them the strength to struggle on. It was to no avail. The surrounded Russians refused to surrender. Chuikov's 62nd Army was now reduced to a dozen isolated outposts, but it was still fighting on. Stalemate had set in. Men were still being killed by the hundred, but the front lines were static and neither side had any hope of securing their hold on the heap of smoking rubble that had once been Stalingrad.

Zeitzler had also been concerned about the Romanian position. He urged Weichs to take steps to strengthen it. A few days later Weichs told the OKH that the 48th Panzer Corps had been moved into position behind the Don so that it could move quickly to plug any gap that opened up in the Romanian front line. This was not such a boost to the Romanians as might be supposed.

The corps was composed of the 14th Panzer Division, the 24th Panzer Division, the 29th Panzergrenadier Division and the 108th Artillery. All of these units had been heavily engaged in the street fighting in Stalingrad. They had been pulled out of the city because they had been judged to be no longer fit for frontline fighting, and were due to be put into reserve until such time as they could be re-equipped and furnished with new recruits.

On 10 November the 48th Panzer Corps reported that it had only 147 operational tanks, barely a third of its full complement. Of these, 92 were the obsolete Panzer 38(T) model, a light tank which would be withdrawn from service in 1943. These were actually Czech tanks that had been grabbed by the Germans in 1939 and pressed into service as reconnaissance vehicles for panzer units, and for dealing with infantry positions. Only 55 of the unit's tanks, the Panzer IV models, stood any chance against the Soviet T34 – and their crews were so tired from the fighting in Stalingrad that they needed serious rest.

Also in need of rest was General Paulus, commander of the 6th Army. His doctor became so concerned that he put in writing that if Paulus did not take a break from command soon he would suffer a breakdown. Paulus told him that he could not take a break at once, but would do so when the campaign ended for the winter. As with Antonescu's meeting with Hitler it would come too late.

The Germans in Stalingrad were running out of time.

9
THE RACE FOR OIL

The whole point of the entire southern campaign in 1942 was supposed to be the drive to capture the Caucasus oilfields. Hitler had been told by his economic advisers that the German war effort could not be maintained on the strength of Romanian oil alone, and so the capture of the Caucasus became the key objective for 1942. And yet the drive to the Caucasus was never properly completed. The reasons for that, and the impact the failure had on the Stalingrad campaign, have been generally overlooked.

List's advance

The Caucasus campaign was the responsibility of Army Group A, commanded by Field Marshal Wilhelm von List. In fact, List was a fairly late arrival to the plan. He had been commanding German forces in Greece until he was summoned to take command of Army Group A, and did not arrive until July 1942, by which time much of the planning had already been completed by Bock, who had been removed by Hitler.

The original plan for Army Group A had been for a drive to Armavir and Maikop on the northern edge of the western Caucasus. The forces would then pause there until Army Group B had secured the northern flank along the Don and the Volga before pushing on southeast to Grozny and the main oilfields. This relatively modest plan was abandoned in April after Hitler and the OKW had got over the shock of the Russian offensive at Moscow in December 1941 and the Germans had regained the initiative.

The new plan called for Army Group A to advance without pause to Grozny and Baku. To carry out this task, List was given the 1st Panzer Army, under Kleist, the 11th Army, the 17th Army (all German units) and the 4th Romanian Army. The force was not as strong as it looked. Although the 11th Army was officially part of Army Group A, it was in fact detached at Hitler's specific command to lay siege to the great Russian naval base of Sevastopol in the Crimea. Under its talented commander, Erich von Manstein, the army was tied up in the siege as the campaign opened. List hoped that Manstein and his army would soon finish the siege and rejoin the bulk of Army Group A in the Caucasus.

In the event, Sevastopol surrendered on 4 July, just days before the drive to the Caucasus was due to begin. Manstein began organizing his army to march east. It would leave the Crimea by crossing the Kerch Strait and arrive behind the Russian left flank as List began his advance. List himself suggested that the 11th Army should march north out of the Crimea and form up behind the Army Group A advance, to act as a mobile reserve. He could then use it wherever the unfolding events of the campaign indicated it would be best deployed. But Hitler stepped in to block both ideas.

Hitler ordered that Manstein and the bulk of the 11th Army should go north by train to join the assault on Leningrad. A division was sent to bolster Army Group Centre, but only a few units were sent to List. The loss of almost half of his infantry strength was a blow to List, but he pressed on with his planning.

List's plan, as it finally emerged, was for the 17th Army to march on the right flank so that the coast of the Sea of Azov lay to its right. The main blow would be struck by the 1st Panzer Army to the north, on the left of the 17th Army. The panzers would punch through the Soviet lines, then hook south by way of Millerovo to reach the Don, east of Rostov. This, List hoped, would envelop the entire Soviet southern sector, forcing the Russian 12th, 18th and 56th Armies either to retreat in haste or be captured. Once the crucial transportation hub of Rostov had been seized, List planned to power rapidly southeast to Armavir and Maikop, then on to Grozny and eventually Baku on the Caspian coast.

The Black Sea coast on his right flank played no part in these plans. List intended simply to isolate the Russian troops along this coast, block the mountain passes by which they could interfere with his plans and then leave them alone. He similarly had no plans to go over the Caucasus Mountains into Georgia, Armenia or Azerbaijan. These Soviet provinces had no oil and little economic value. Again the mountain passes could be blocked with ease and Soviet forces south of the mountains ignored.

More problematic was the vast Kalmyk Steppe. This huge area of dry grassland stretched from the lower Volga to the Caucasus and covered around 103,000 square kilometres (40,000 square miles). The land had no intrinsic worth and was sparsely inhabited by nomadic herders, but it did expose much of the left wing of List's intended advance.

If Weichs and Army Group B secured the lower Volga, then the Kalmyk would not pose much of a threat, but if the lower Volga remained in Soviet hands the Soviets might feed reinforcements over the

Kalmyk to attack List's flank. List opted to send strong motorized patrols out into the Kalmyk to see what was going on there, but to make no attempt to occupy it.

Panzer fuel problems

List's advance got under way as Weichs was marching on Voronezh. Weichs' actions also served to keep the Soviet high command focused on that area and make them think that the Germans were planning to attack Moscow from the south.

Kleist's panzers punched through the disorganized Soviet forces in front of them as planned and motored on, meeting very little opposition. The 17th Army duly advanced on the right flank, again without encountering much trouble. As we have seen, Hoth's 4th Panzer Army was diverted away from Stalingrad to help Kleist capture Rostov, when he could have managed perfectly well on his own.

On 25 July Kleist crossed the river and two days later recommenced his drive towards the oilfields, Hoth being sent back north towards Stalingrad. Kleist's panzers could then really get into their stride. The landscape was open, and devoid of large towns to slow them down. On 19 July he captured Proletarskaya, on 31 July Salsk fell, and on 7 August his leading tanks rolled into Armavir. Just two days later the first Russian oil wells were captured as Kleist's panzers swarmed over the area around Maikop. On the same day other panzers reached the foothills of the Caucasus at Pyatigorsk, 240 kilometres (150 miles) east of Maikop, while light motorized units scouting at speed into the Kalmyk got to Budennovsk another 160 kilometres (100 miles) east. It was one of the fastest German advances of the entire war.

Behind Kleist, the 17th Army under General Richard Ruoff captured Rostov and then followed in the tracks of Kleist's tanks. Ruoff successfully performed his task of mopping up the pockets of resistance left behind by Kleist's fast-moving panzers. The Russians blew the huge dam on the Manych River, hoping to disrupt German supply lines, but after a pause of only two days the advance went on.

The panzers, meanwhile, had run into serious trouble. It was not the Soviets that were the problem, at least not directly, but the Soviet railway system. List had been planning to use the long Russian railway line from Rostov to Baku via Grozny to supply his armies. But things were not that easy. For a start the bottleneck at the junction at Rostov limited how much freight could be handled, while the problems with the different Russian gauges proved to cause even more delays than List's railway engineers had anticipated.

Writing after the war, Kleist lamented the situation.

'The primary cause of our failure was shortage of petrol. The bulk of our supplies had to come by rail from the Rostov bottleneck, as the Black Sea route was considered unsafe. A certain amount of fuel was delivered by air, but the total which came through was insufficient to maintain the momentum of the advance, which came to a halt just when our chances looked best.'

Kleist was correct. At this date the Soviet defences were almost non-existent. If his panzers had been given enough fuel they could have driven almost unopposed all the way to Baku.

But they did not have the petrol, and the delay gave the Soviet commander, Semyon Budenny, time to organize and bring in reinforcements. Although Budenny did well in reorganizing his defences, Stalin had still not forgiven him for the disaster at Kiev in 1941 and soon replaced him with Ivan Petrov.

List grinds to a halt

List, meanwhile, had divided his front into two. Kleist's 1st Panzer Army was responsible for the Kalmyk Steppe and for the drive along the foothills of the Caucasus to Grozny and Baku. The 17th Army was to advance down the Black Sea coast to capture the ports of Tuapse and Batum. It was here that the Russian Black Sea Fleet was ready to sally out and attack the supply convoys from Romania that kept List's men in fuel, ammunition and food. If the ports could be captured, the fleet would

---

have no choice but to steam to neutral Turkish ports and be interned for the duration. This would allow German supply ships to use the Black Sea, which would ease the bottleneck at Rostov.

Unfortunately for the 17th Army, the terrain over which it was supposed to advance was composed of precipitous cliffs, towering peaks, hidden ravines and hopelessly inadequate tracks that were misleadingly marked as roads on the few maps available.

The campaign soon degenerated into a series of bitterly fought infantry actions in terrible terrain. By October the 17th Army had still not advanced the 120 kilometres (75 miles) to Tuapse.

Kleist was forced to wait until he had built up stocks of fuel and ammunition before resuming his advance. The Terek River, flowing down from the mountains out to the Kalmyk, proved to be a difficult obstacle. Its current was swift and its bed was both deep and broken, while the Soviets were now dug in on the far side. Repeated thrusts in late August failed to break the river line, but in early September the panzers got across further downstream at Mozdok. The huge oilfield at Grozny was now only 80 kilometres (50 miles) away.

Even at this moment of potential triumph, Kleist had more problems. Once again writing after the war he explained,

'Bad though the lack of fuel was, it was not the ultimate cause of failure. We could still have reached our goal (Baku) if my forces had not been drawn away bit by bit to help the attack on Stalingrad. Besides part of my motorized infantry, I had to give up all of my flak corps and all my air force, except for some reconnaissance squadrons. These losses contributed to what, in my opinion, was a further cause of failure. The Russians suddenly concentrated a force of 800 bombers on my front, operating from airfields near Grozny. Although only about a third of these bombers were modern, they sufficed to put a brake on my continued advance. This was all the more effective because of my lack of fighters and flak.'

Not only that, but the failure of Army Group B to secure the lower Volga meant that Russian supplies and reinforcements could flow unhindered to bolster the Soviet defences. As Kleist later recalled, the Soviet forces did not restrict themselves to defensive fighting, but also launched raids and nuisance attacks.

'The Russians brought reserves from Siberia. These developed a menace to my flank here [on the Kalmyk Steppe] which was so widely stretched that the Russian cavalry could always penetrate my outposts whenever they chose. This flank concentration of theirs was helped by the railway that the Russians had built across the steppe from Astrakhan south. It was roughly laid, straight over the level plain without any foundation. Efforts to deal with the menace by wrecking the railway proved useless for as soon as any section of railway was destroyed a fresh set of rails was quickly laid down. My patrols reached the Caspian many times, but that advance took us nowhere for my forces in the steppe were

striking against an intangible foe. As time passed and the Russian strength grew in that area the flanking menace became increasingly serious.'

A Russian newspaper correspondent named Eugene Krueger was riding with the cavalry on the Kalmyk Steppe at the time, and recorded his impressions.

'The day was drawing to a close when the General returned from the front. Without pausing to take off his jacket he walked over to the table and unfolded a map. He proceeded to explain the situation and the plan for subsequent operations. His speech was quick, laconic. Giving little time to minor detail, he tried to make everybody present understand his main idea. His enthusiasm was contagious, his speech rough.

'I asked him about the weapons his cavalry use. He replied, "Rifle, sabre, grenade, petrol bombs. Look at this man" – he pointed at a grey-bearded officer sitting nearby eating – "Queer chap. He once

attacked a tank from his horse. What am I meant to do with him? But he got a grenade into the tank and killed the crew. That old boy is the real stuff."

'The General told me that his Cossacks took no baggage train with them on a raid, but carried everything they needed on their own horses. He told me of one raid. After infiltrating the German lines the men rode for 60 miles [96 kilometres] into the enemy territory. There they became complete masters of the situation, damaging roads and communications, burning stores and destroying lorries and trucks. They harried the enemy without respite. On the second day they ran into a German infantry formation and destroyed it. Then the Cossacks split up into small groups and scattered in all directions to evade pursuit.

'For 12 days they rode around behind Fascist lines, then they came home. They had destroyed 250 German soldiers, 87 machine-guns, 115 lorries, two ammunition dumps and three radio stations.

'Another incident worth reporting came when

a Cossack force was pinned down by Germans in a ravine. The Cossack commander had to send for reinforcements and chose his five best riders for the job, hoping one at least would get through. Each was given a sealed envelope with the same message. They made for gaps in the German lines, but were in full view of the German soldiers. In a moment no less than ten machine-guns opened up on the horsemen. One by one the Cossack riders fell from their saddles, trailing lifeless from the stirrup as their horses dragged the men over the ground. All five messages seemed to be lost. But it was just a Cossack trick. As soon as the horses were out of sight of the Germans, the seemingly dead riders sprang back into the saddle. All five messages were safely delivered.'

By late August, List's advance had ground to a halt on both of his fronts. With the autumn weather drawing in, the prospect of either securing the main oilfields or forcing the Soviet fleet into internment before winter arrived looked increasingly poor. Coupled with the failure to capture Stalingrad, the delays in the Caucasus infuriated Hitler. He sent List three new divisions, along with orders to strike over the western end of the mountain chain and attack Batum from the landward side. As was usual when Hitler originated an idea, he had the staff at the OKH work out the details under his own supervision, then sent them to List to be carried out exactly as specified, with no leeway to adapt them to local conditions.

When the attack failed in the face of difficult terrain and determined Soviet resistance, Hitler became increasingly impatient for results and dismissive of List. In early September Hitler sent Jodl, Chief of Operations at the OKW, to List's headquarters, both to express his displeasure and to order List to get a move on. Jodl stayed a couple of days while he inspected List's dispositions and supply situation. He came away realizing that the chances of achieving the campaign's objectives were slim.

When Jodl returned to Hitler's headquarters he

went to his desk to prepare his notes for the meeting with Hitler and the rest of the general staff, at which he would report on his trip. Hitler was too impatient to wait for the meeting and went over to talk to Jodl. Hitler listened as Jodl outlined the situation and the poor prospects in the area. He then launched into one of his monologues, reciting his by then usual diatribes about the inability of his generals to understand his vision and the poor quality of the senior military staff. He ended by stating that List should have attacked at a single point, not spread his forces among several different mountain passes.

'But, my Führer,' said Jodl, in a move he was going to regret for a long time, 'he did exactly what he was ordered to do.'

Jodl then pointed to the orders from the OKW that had instructed List to attack as he had done. At the bottom of the covering note to the orders was the signature of Hitler himself.

Hitler looked at the orders bearing his signature and went white. He stared speechless at Jodl as utter silence fell on the busy room. His eyes bulging in fury, Hitler turned on his heel and stalked away from the meeting.

Hitler takes control of Army Group A

It was this incident that caused Hitler to consider Paulus as a replacement for Jodl. Although Jodl was not replaced, and remained in position to the end of the war, Hitler was cool to him for some months, and it is arguable that Hitler never again trusted Jodl. But the split with Jodl had implications far beyond the two men concerned. Writing after the war, Jodl's deputy Walter Warlimont, explained:

'Further consequences were that Hitler completely changed his daily routine. From that time on he stayed away from the communal meals that until then he had taken twice a day with his entourage and the OKW officers. Henceforth he hardly left his offices in daytime, not even for the daily reports on the military situation from the army commanders,

which from then on had to be delivered to him in his own hut in the presence of a narrowly restricted circle. He refused ostentatiously to shake hands with any general of the OKW.

'Jodl on one of the rare occasions when he confided in me was inclined to find an explanation for Hitler's extreme reaction to this event in the psychological field. Jodl had concluded that a dictator, as a matter of psychological necessity, must never be reminded of his own errors – in order to keep up his self-confidence, the ultimate source of his dictatorial force.

'My own opinion was and is plainer, but reaches farther. I am convinced that Hitler, when confronted with the actual situation at the end of the second offensive against Russia, suddenly grasped that he would never reach his goal in the East and that the war would eventually be lost.'

Whatever the reasons for Hitler's reaction, his next move was swift and sudden. List was sacked and replaced by

Hitler himself. Of course, Hitler had no intention of going to southern Russia to take up his new position, nor of relinquishing his existing duties as Führer of the German government and Commander-in-Chief of the German armed forces. He did not have time to run Army Group A at all. For the next few weeks Kleist and Ruoff found themselves ignored when they needed decisions made, or deluged with orders and demands for information when they would have preferred to have been left alone.

It would be November before Hitler relinquished his nominal command of Army Group A and appointed Kleist to take over. Kleist was in turn replaced as commander of the 1st Panzer Army by Eberhard von Mackensen.

By that date there had not been much movement on the Caucasus Front. Propaganda chief Josef Goebbels had filmed some German mountaineers scaling Mount Elbrus, which at 5,642 metres (18,510 feet) is the tallest peak in Europe, and Kleist had made a series of half-hearted efforts to break out from his advanced positions around Mozdok, but otherwise not much had happened. The Soviets seemed content merely to watch the Germans, while launching a few raids on the extended German supply system.

It was almost as if they were waiting for something.

10
OPERATION URANUS

There had been signs for weeks, for those willing to see them. As early as September General Günther Blumentritt, Chief Quartermaster of the OKH, had written a report on the position at Stalingrad that had concluded, 'It would not be safe to hold such a long defensive flank during the winter.' In October the Romanian commander General Petre Dumitrescu had produced a report predicting a large Russian attack against his troops. In early November even Kurt Zeitzler, Chief of Staff at the OKH, had tentatively suggested that it was time to think about finding an easily defended position in which to spend the winter.

Casualties mount

And yet the 6th Army stayed in Stalingrad, battering at Soviet defences and paying a high price in blood. The attacks were now much smaller than before, little more than company-strength aggressive patrolling, but they still cost men their lives. It was not just the Russians that were causing casualties. The 6th Army began to suffer a disproportionately high rate of disease, no doubt brought on by a combination of stress, low morale and poor rations. Dysentery and typhus were particular problems.

The main reason why the 6th Army had stayed in Stalingrad was that Hitler and his senior staff officers had fatally misread the signs. They believed that the main Soviet strength was much further north, around Rzhev, and that the expected Russian winter onslaught would take place there. Russian activity around Stalingrad had been seen as an indication of a relatively small-scale offensive, designed to lure German forces out of the city and so relieve pressure on Chuikov and his battered 62nd Army. Paulus, Weichs and Hitler were all convinced that a Russian attack would take place somewhere near Stalingrad, and they were all equally certain that it would be on a small scale and easily contained.

Soviet counterattack plans

In fact, the Soviets had been quietly and methodically building up their forces for a counterattack at Stalingrad on a grand scale. The plan had been devised on 13 September when Zhukov had gone to Moscow to meet Stalin and his chief of staff, Aleksandr Vasilevsky. Zhukov and Vasilevsky had concocted a plan to launch simultaneous attacks on the Romanian troops who held the line on either side of the German 6th Army. These incursions would drive fast and deep to link up behind the 6th Army and cut it off. They believed that the Red Army had enough strength to mount the strikes, but nothing more. All other planned operations would have to be cancelled and all reserves would take part in what was dubbed Operation Uranus.

After some hesitation, Stalin accepted the plan.

He gave Vasilevsky authority to move, equip and train whatever forces were necessary for the plan. But Stalin imposed one condition: absolute secrecy. Nobody, but nobody, was to be told the reason for the changes and movements. If anyone asked they were to be fobbed off with vague comments about limited local actions. Each commander would be kept in ignorance of the fact that his forces were to act as part of a larger enterprise. Only as the time for the offensive drew nearer were a small number of senior planning and command staff to be let in on the secret.

As they drew up their plans in secret, Zhukov and Vasilevsky decided on a major change in tactics. They decided, so far as was possible, to copy the Germans' blitzkrieg tactics. Russian tactical doctrine had previously emphasized the importance of units keeping in touch with those on their flanks and advancing only when their flanks were known to be secure. Now Zhukov began instructing his tank commanders to push forward far and fast, irrespective of what was happening on their flanks. Infantry commanders were told that their new task was to follow the tanks, not lead the assault. Cavalry officers were ordered to abandon their hit and run tactics. Instead they were to ride with the tanks, dismounting to fight as infantry when required. Air units were instructed to co-operate closely with their ground forces, especially the tanks. Not only that, but Zhukov's plan called for a massive concentration of force in a small area to achieve the initial breakthrough, what the Germans termed the *Schwerpunkt*.

It is true that Soviet equipment was not as suited to this sort of fast-moving offensive as that of the Germans. For a start, many Soviet tanks lacked radios. Even more restricting was the poor state of the Soviet supply system, which meant that the tanks would lose touch with their sources of fuel and ammunition relatively quickly. But then Operation Uranus did not call for an extended tank drive such as those the Germans had carried out in 1941. The overall aim was rather less ambitious, and was within Soviet capabilities.

The Uranus offensive would be launched at three *Schwerpunkt*. The first was to be at Kletskaya, to the west of Stalingrad. The aim of this drive was to smash a hole in the Romanian front, then swing round to face the Germans outside Stalingrad and keep them occupied. Meanwhile the main attack would be launched further west at Serafimovich, about 160 kilometres (100 miles) from Stalingrad. This offensive was to smash through the Romanians and then race southeast towards Kalach, driving a deep and expanding wedge into the rear of the Romanian 3rd Army. A final attack was to be launched to the south of Stalingrad at Plodovitoye. This advance was intended to be deep and fast too, with the target also being Kalach. When the columns met at Kalach the Germans in Stalingrad would be surrounded and trapped.

Zhukov and Vasilevsky estimated that the offensive capabilities of the Red Army would then have been exhausted. The Soviets would then go over to the defensive to hold the ground they had won and prevent the trapped 6th Army from escaping. Given enough time, Zhukov estimated, Paulus and his men would be starved into surrender.

The training and preparations went on for weeks, but it was not until late in October that the men and equipment began to be moved towards Stalingrad. At the same time, those in the front lines were ordered to carry out more intensive patrolling and scouting, to ascertain the dispositions of the Romanians and the details of the landscape over which the attacks would be taking place. It was this increased activity that had alarmed Dumitrescu and prompted him to submit his report to Weichs.

The movements of the Soviet forces were carried out under the utmost secrecy. Each individual unit knew where it was going, but was oblivious of other movements. Russian prisoners and deserters told the Romanians and the Germans about their own regiments, but that was all. Strenuous efforts were made to hide the build-up from roving *Luftwaffe* pilots. All troop movements took place at night, with the troops and their equipment remaining motionless under camouflage during the day. There was also a lot of false activity going on. All along the front where the offensive was to take place the Russian soldiers were kept busy constructing elaborate defensive works and building comfortable huts to give the impression that they were intending to stay put for the winter. Zhukov estimated that he needed 5 new bridges over the Don to supply his offensive, but to disguise their importance he had 17 new bridges built elsewhere. Then the rains came, followed by bitter frosts.

The delays imposed by the need for secrecy and by the bad weather meant that Operation Uranus had to be deferred by ten days, to 19 November. On 13 November Zhukov travelled to Moscow to give a final and detailed briefing to Stalin and Vasilevsky. There was some concern about the strength of the *Luftwaffe* in the area, but in the end no changes were made to the plans. Snow fell over Stalingrad that day and the Russian troops were issued with their white uniforms. On 14 November there was a scare when a patrol came back to report that there were German troops in the Romanian sector near Kletskaya. Zhukov worried that the Germans had got wind of the coming attack and had replaced the weak Romanian units with new German ones. In fact the Germans were engineers come to give the Romanians advice on building dugouts. Later patrols failed to find any more Germans and the scare faded.

The 6th Army is surrounded

At 4 am on 19 November the Russian troops were woken up and given their orders. They had long suspected that an attack was imminent, but not until this late hour did they realize just what was involved. When the tank crews were told they were to plunge so deep and so fast behind the German lines they cheered. The attack was to begin at 7 am – dawn. When the sun came up there was a dense, freezing fog. The attack began on schedule.

Zhukov had assembled a huge force for his attack. He had nine armies, more than a million men, 13,000 guns, 894 tanks and 1,150 aircraft. The size of the effort is shown by the fact that two thirds of all Soviet tanks in operational condition were thrown into the offensive.

The artillery opened up first, swamping the Romanian positions with the heaviest and longest Soviet artillery barrage of the war to date. The Russian artillery was usually accurate, but barrages rarely lasted long, due to a lack of ammunition. There was no such problem on this day and the guns roared continuously.

In Stalingrad, the men on both sides heard the continuous roar of guns and wondered what it heralded. Among those in the dark was Chuikov himself. At 2 am he had received a radio message instructing him to stand by for important news, but even he did not know what was going on.

The Romanians might have been equipped with outdated weapons, and perhaps lacked training in up-to-date tactics, but they knew how to dig trenches. The great Soviet artillery barrage had much less effect than had been hoped. The first Russian attack, mounted by infantry, was beaten off in most places. The Soviet generals knew that speed was essential, so they sent in the T34 tanks to support their infantry for the second attack. At noon the Romanians gave way at Kletskaya, and at 3 pm they were overrun at Serafimovich.

Adhering to their new orders to plunge fast and far into enemy territory, the Soviet tanks pushed on with cavalry support. Their rapid advance threw the Romanian rear areas into confusion. Like the French army in 1940 they were simply not equipped to cope with the dislocation to communications and supply lines that a fast tank thrust caused. Units were separated from their headquarters, supply dumps were destroyed and communication systems ceased to function.

It was not until almost 10 am that a telephone call got through to Paulus at 6th Army headquarters to tell him that a Russian attack was under way on the Romanian positions. He already knew that, having been listening to the artillery barrage for some time. What he needed was details, but none were forthcoming. At 11 am the 48th Panzer Corps, the key reserve unit, was ordered to move north to tackle some Russian tanks of unknown type and quantity. It was reported that they had broken through the Romanians and were advancing toward Gromky.

In Stalingrad, Paulus chose to wait for firm news before doing anything. Crucially he left the 16th Panzer Division in the city rather than ordering it out of the ruins to form up for action in the open countryside. Darkness fell at 4 pm and an hour later the leading Soviet tanks of the 5th Tank Army blundered into the lead elements of the 48th Panzer Corps. The fighting was disorganized and chaotic, but at least the German crews were able to radio out an accurate description of the Soviet strength and position. At 6 pm Paulus ordered all attacks in the city to halt, then pulled his tanks out, sending them west towards the Don. There was not enough fuel immediately available and a delay of some hours followed while the panzers made a detour to collect petrol from Rynok. Paulus told his panzer commanders not to go too far. The Romanian area was not his direct concern, so he contented himself with guarding his rear, not with stopping the Soviet blitzkrieg.

At dawn next day the Russian southern attack was launched and by mid-morning it had got through the Romanian 18th Division near Sarpa. The Russians began to drive ahead fast, but in the early afternoon they ran headlong into the 29th Panzergrenadier Division and were brought to a sudden halt. This division had been in reserve south of Stalingrad and had moved further south on hearing the artillery barrage. However its commander, General Hans-Georg Leyser, had no real orders from Paulus so he dug in to either await orders or renewed Soviet attacks. The Russians, realizing that the Germans would be too tough to overcome quickly, changed direction to sweep around the panzergrenadiers.

To the northwest, the main Soviet advance was proceeding as planned. The units of the 48th Panzer Corps had become confused by the contradictory orders reaching them and by the incoherent reports coming in about Soviet positions and movements. The 22nd Panzer Division, finding itself entirely surrounded, blasted a path through the Soviet positions and a handful of survivors got away to the southwest. Meanwhile the Romanian units cut off by the Soviet advance were digging in under the command of General Mihail Lascăr.

On the morning of 21 November, the second day of the operation, Paulus prepared to send his remaining panzers to assault the left flank of the Russian columns advancing from Kletskaya. Before the attack could be delivered he heard that Soviet tanks were only 32 kilometres (20 miles) from his headquarters and that another Soviet column was surging northwest from his southern flank. Paulus suddenly realized that his entire army was in danger of encirclement. Just as urgent, most of his supply and support units were in the path of the rapidly advancing Soviets. Orders were hurriedly sent out alerting them to the danger and telling them to get to safety as fast as possible. He himself abandoned his headquarters, as staff tried to pack up papers and equipment, and headed east to Stalingrad. A new headquarters was established at Gumrak.

The Soviet advance continued after dark as the Germans were thrown into confusion, with units heading in different directions under different orders from different commanders. At 6 am a Soviet tank column coming from the north reached Kalach. Finding no sign of their comrades coming from the east, the tank crews pushed on and at dawn saw T34 tanks advancing towards them. The encirclement was complete. The 6th Army was surrounded.

Chaos and confusion

The Soviets continued to pour into their newly captured territory, widening the strip of land they had won. The German and Romanian retreat was, in places, chaotic as men separated from their units surged towards the rear. Elsewhere regiments or companies fought effective rearguard actions. But there was no stopping the Russian advance. It could only be delayed.

In places, German and Romanian prisoners were killed by Soviet troops. It was a grim foretaste of the vengeance the Russians were to inflict on those who had invaded their country. The NKVD operatives following the Red Army were every bit as ruthless.

Any civilian who had helped the Germans in any way was first arrested and questioned, then shot. At least 750 were thus executed in the first week of the Russian operation, often on no more evidence than the say so of a neighbour.

While chaos and confusion engulfed the Romanians and the Germans around Stalingrad, things were not much better among the German high command. On the evening of 19 November, Zeitzler seems to have recognized that the Russian attack was a major one. He telephoned Hitler, who was at his Alpine holiday retreat at Berchtesgaden, to give him the news. Next day Hitler issued a stream of orders. The first was for Manstein, formerly commander of the 11th Army, to leave Leningrad and head back south to take control of the situation. The second was for General Ferdinand Heim, the hapless commander of the 48th Panzer Corps, to be arrested on unspecified charges. Finally he ordered Paulus to take command of all units on his side of the Soviet thrusts, and to hold firm while the situation was sorted out.

Paulus telephoned around his corps commanders on the afternoon of 22 November, to ask their views on the rapidly changing situation. They were unanimous. The 6th Army had to abandon Stalingrad and break out southwest to rejoin the rest of Army Group B. Paulus radioed at 7 pm, asking permission for the move. The reply from Hitler came at 10 pm. It read:

> '*The 6th Army is temporarily surrounded by Russian forces. I know the 6th Army and your commander in chief and have no doubt that in this difficult situation it will hold on bravely. The 6th Army must know that I am doing everything to relieve them. I will issue my orders in good time. Adolf Hitler.*'

Uncertain what to make of this enigmatic message, but convinced that a break-out was the only sensible option, Paulus began issuing orders for an attack southwest, to punch through the encircling troops.

Having issued his order, Hitler set out to return to his headquarters. He stopped every few hours to telephone Zeitzler for an update. Zeitzler, with his background in logistics, had very rapidly come to the conclusion that if the 6th Army did not break out soon it was doomed. There were not enough supplies in Stalingrad to keep the 22 divisions going until the spring. Air supply was out of the question. The *Luftwaffe* had done well supplying a few isolated divisions over the previous winter, but keeping an entire army supplied was impossible. He did some quick calculations. The 6th Army had three weeks, probably less.

Meanwhile, Field Marshal Erich von Manstein, previously commander of the 11th Army, was also on the move. He too stopped frequently to make telephone calls. He had been put in temporary command of the Army Group Don, which consisted of the 6th Army, the 1st Panzer Army and the 3rd Romanian Army. His task was to stabilize the situation. He brought with him most of the administration staff of the old 11th Army, who he had managed to keep with him, but little else.

On his journey south, Manstein came to recognize the disastrous situation that awaited him. Of the forces under his command the 6th Army was trapped in Stalingrad; the 3rd Romanian army was reduced to only two infantry divisions, because the rest of its men were dead, scattered or trapped in Stalingrad; and the 4th Panzer Army was likewise partly in Stalingrad and partly outside the trap.

On 23 November, Manstein told Zeitzler that he needed the equivalent of a full army to accomplish his task. A few hours later Zeitzler radioed back that he could promise three divisions, one armoured and two infantry. It was not enough.

On the following day, 24 November, Manstein reached the headquarters of Army Group B and had a long meeting with Weichs. He then had an equally lengthy telephone conversation with Zeitzler. That same day Hitler reached his command headquarters, and was briefed at length by Zeitzler and other senior staff officers.

The precise sequence of events on that crucial 24

November is hotly disputed. The results of the decisions reached turned out to be so utterly disastrous for the 6th Army and for Germany that nobody wanted to take the blame. After the war, the senior officers involved were all keen to pin the blame on Hitler, who was by then officially dead. It is possible, however, to put together what might have happened by combining the post-war accounts with the contemporary records.

To break out or not?

It seems clear that by the afternoon of 23 November the initial confusion about what was going on had passed. It was by now evident to the Germans that the 6th Army was surrounded and that the Soviets had deployed a massively larger and more competent force than the Germans had thought possible. The various meetings and telephone calls that took place on 24 November represented the Germans' first opportunity to come to a considered decision about what to do. Up until then they had been merely reacting to events in a rushed and haphazard fashion.

The first meeting was almost certainly that between *Luftwaffe* chief Hermann Goering and the heads of his transport section. Goering had fallen out with Hitler a year earlier, when he had pointedly reminded Hitler in front of others that he had been opposed to invading Russia, and had predicted that the Soviets could not be defeated in a single summer.

He had rehabilitated himself slightly in the months that followed, when the *Luftwaffe* had supplied trapped divisions in Russia and had kept up the pressure on the Soviets with effective bombing raids. Now Goering saw a chance to get fully back into the Führer's favour.

He had only one question for his transport officers. Could the *Luftwaffe* keep the 6th Army supplied by air throughout the winter? The officers did their sums, then told Goering that they could promise to deliver 350 tons of supplies each day for a month, but no longer. After that date the transport aircraft would need to be stood down for maintenance and repairs. And that estimate was dependent on the Soviet fighters not interfering.

Goering then telephoned Jans Jeschonnek, the *Luftwaffe* officer on Hitler's personal staff, and told him that the *Luftwaffe* could supply 500 tons per day for the forseeable future. Jeschonnek in turn reported this gross overestimation of the *Luftwaffe*'s abilities to Hitler's meeting with Zeitzler. As a good logistics officer, Zeitzler had a shrewd idea of what the 6th Army would need by way of supplies. He estimated that a minimum of 750 tons per day would be required to keep Paulus and his men fighting. There seems to have been a fairly lengthy discussion about what could be achieved on 500 tons per day.

The discussion then moved on to the vexed question of what Manstein and Paulus should do. There were two basic options under discussion – at least so far as anyone would later admit. The first possibility was that Paulus should try to break out at once, while Manstein launched an attack on the Russians with whatever he had to hand. This plan had the advantage that the Russians would be rather disorganized after their rapid advance, and would not yet have had the chance to construct proper defensive positions. On the other hand the 6th Army was arranged with its best units facing Stalingrad, and only weaker or reserve units facing outwards. Any attack they made would be scrappy and probably not very well organized. And Manstein's forces were at that point even less prepared to mount an offensive.

Alternatively, the break-out attempt could be delayed for ten days or so. This would give Paulus the time to get his best units into position to lead the break-out, while Manstein would by then have received his promised reinforcements. Against these advantages had to be weighed the fact that the Russians would by then have had time to strengthen their defences.

By coincidence this was the day fixed for Hitler's meeting with the Romanian leader Antonescu. The meeting opened with Antonescu trying to give an up-to-date account of where his men were and how many had survived. He had barely begun when Hitler interrupted him. The Führer launched into a tirade blaming the Romanian 4th Army for the disaster. He claimed that they were incapable of fighting a decent battle. Antonescu responded by blaming Hitler for not having listened to the warnings given by General Dumitrescu some three weeks earlier. Within minutes the meeting had degenerated into an unseemly shouting match. Antonescu stormed out and it was left to staff officers to find a face-saving form of words to describe the meeting. Antonescu went back to Bucharest and when the full scale of the disaster to his men was revealed he suffered a breakdown.

At some point Manstein telephoned Zeitzler from Weichs' headquarters. He had also been having discussions about Stalingrad, this time with Weichs and his staff, and moreover had been given an on-the-spot briefing as to the latest situation in the area. The conversation ranged over the two options of attempting a break-out at once or trying one later. Manstein was of the opinion that if they went for an immediate move there would be very high casualties. He believed that most of the panzer units would get out, along with the panzergrenadiers in their motorized vehicles – and anyone else who could get on to a lorry or into a car – but he thought that the infantry were probably doomed. Their only chance would be to stay put and wait for a better organized break-out attempt.

Speaking after the war, Manstein claimed that he had then emphasized that if the 6th Army did not have ample supplies in Stalingrad already, or could not be kept supplied somehow, an immediate break-out was necessary, despite the risks.

According to most later accounts, it was Hitler who objected to the break-out. He was determined to hold on to the gains won in southern Russia during the summer and refused to countenance retreat. It was Hitler, those who survived the war later claimed, who had been intransigent and blind to reality. It was Hitler who insisted that Paulus and the 6th Army had to stay put and fight it out. Undoubtedly, Hitler did prefer this option. The embarrassment of retreating so soon after his regime had announced to the world that Stalingrad would be taken would have been a grievous political blow. Moreover, Hitler had refused to retreat in the face of the Soviet offensive at Moscow in December 1941, and this decision had proved to be right. Now he once again opposed retreat. But for all his faults Hitler was not a complete fool. In any case, by the time this version of events came out he was dead and therefore easy to blame.

The Army Group A issue

What neither Manstein, Weichs, Zeitzler nor any of the other staff officers at these meetings ever mentioned was that there was another and very pressing issue that they were all aware of, and which could not be ignored. That was the fate of Army Group A. By surrounding Stalingrad, the Soviets had shown that they had more men, more tanks, more guns and better tactical organization than the Germans had ever imagined. On 24 November nobody on the German side knew if Operation Uranus represented the full extent of the Soviets' plans. It might have been merely the first step in an even greater offensive. If the Soviets were now to turn southwest down the Don they could conceivably reach Rostov in less than a week. That would mean that the whole of Army Group A would be cut off. It would then not only be the 6th Army at risk, but the 17th Army, the 1st Panzer Army and several other units as well. We know now that the Russians did not have the strength to attempt this move, and had no intention of even trying, but nobody on the German side was aware of the fact.

Manstein was the best strategist the Germans had, perhaps the finest in the war as a whole. He at least must have appreciated the danger. The only chance for Army Group A was for the 6th Army to stay in Stalingrad and tie down the Soviet forces there for long enough for the troops to fall back from the Caucasus and get across the Don at Rostov.

If the 6th Army broke out, the Soviets would come on its heels and capture Rostov. Zeitzler, the logistics expert, would have recognized that if the 6th Army could not be kept ticking over by supplying it by air, there was no chance of doing anything for Army Group A in the distant Caucasus. If Kleist and his vast army group was to survive then Paulus had to hold out in Stalingrad for at least two or three weeks, maybe longer.

There is no proof that the fate of Army Group A was ever discussed by anybody on 24 November, but it would be strange indeed if it had not been. Perhaps it was Manstein who raised the subject, but later tried to evade responsibility. We do not know. All we do know is that as a result of whatever discussions did take place Hitler issued an order declaring that Stalingrad was now 'Fortress Stalingrad', and had to be held at all costs.

11
OPERATION WINTER STORM

Whatever the reasons for the decision, Paulus and the 6th Army were ordered to sit tight in the ruins of Stalingrad until Manstein could get a rescue plan together. But the fighting was still going on and it was not at all clear at this stage how long Paulus could hold out.

Waiting to strike

When the Soviet offensive had begun on 19 November, the Soviet commander in Stalingrad, Chuikov, had been taken as much by surprise as Paulus. In the days that followed, Chuikov was likewise instructed to sit tight. He launched no attacks on the Germans, nor were any fresh troops sent to attack the 6th Army, although Zhukov and Yeremenko had plenty in hand. They did not want to push Paulus and his men away from Stalingrad, in case this move became a general retreat that in turn became a break-out attempt. They wanted to keep the 6th Army where it was so that it could be surrounded and destroyed.

That said, the Soviets in the encircling forces needed to make the gap between the 6th Army at Stalingrad and the new German lines on the lower Don so great that no break-out attempt could succeed. To this purpose the Soviets continued to squeeze the western and southern flanks of the 6th Army. What had seemed to be a secure defensive line between 23 and 27 November was pushed back on the 28th and it was not until 30 November that the Soviet advance came to a halt. The Germans and the Romanians in the pocket were now under siege.

Gathering the German forces

Outside Stalingrad, Hitler imposed a complete news blackout on events. Reports of the Russian offensive were published in Germany, but the news articles and newsreels stated that the offensive had been halted. This was true, but no mention was made of the fact that the offensive had not been halted until the 6th Army had been surrounded.

Propaganda chief Josef Goebbels was unhappy with this decision. He had built his enormously successful career on a platform of blending truth and lies with emotions and prejudice, but his key policy had always been to make whatever he said believable, even if it was actually untrue. Goebbels was not convinced that Stalingrad could be saved and was therefore disturbed by the fact that its plight was not to be talked about. He withdrew to think about how he and the Nazi propaganda machine would handle events.

Those events were proceeding quickly. For the 6th Army and its attendant units to break out successfully there were three elements that Manstein had to get in place. The first of these was the force that was to fight its way through the Soviets to reach Paulus and his men. The second was the trapped army itself, which had to be ready to break out and move fast. The third was the Soviet army, which would need to be defeated, or at least pushed aside and kept at bay long enough for the trapped units to escape. None of these elements proved to be easy for Manstein to manage.

The first element, the breakthrough army, was most directly under Manstein's control, since it was forming up around the lower Don where he was based. His first problem was acquiring the forces that he believed he needed. That meant persuading Hitler that there was a need to transfer units from elsewhere, and then inducing their current commanders to let them go.

First to arrive were the survivors of the 48th

Panzer Corps. Although badly battered, they were still effective. That unit, and its headquarters staff, was used as the basis for the formation of a formidable new corps. Then there was the 11th Panzer Division, under its redoubtable commander General Hermann Balck, one of the finer tactical panzer commanders in the army.

The 11th Panzer Division had an eventful journey to join Manstein. On 7 December, as the panzers were travelling north from Rostov, the Soviets launched an armoured thrust with their 5th Guards Tank Army west of Rychkov. Two Soviet brigades got through Manstein's front line and pushed 32 kilometres (20 miles) south. At dusk they met the 11th Panzers coming north and went into defensive positions. Balck manoeuvred his anti-tank guns into a similarly defensive posture, blocking the Soviet route south, then drove his panzers in a great sweeping route to the west, so that they arrived behind the Soviet tanks at dawn. As the sun rose, the Soviets climbed into their tanks and headed south to where they believed the panzers to be. When they ran into the anti-tank guns, the Soviets deployed to attack, at which point Balck attacked them from behind. It was a massacre. Balck reached Manstein triumphant, but his triumph was to be short-lived.

Also sent to join Manstein was the 6th Panzer Division, commanded by General Franz Landgraf. This unit was a formidable, full-strength panzer division. It had fought on the Eastern Front throughout 1941, but after taking serious losses in the Soviet counteroffensive at Moscow it had then been moved to France to recover and to form part of the occupation army. It was now not only at full strength but it was also equipped with the very latest weaponry. After receiving orders to leave France on 24 November, it reached the Don by rail on 8 December. By the time it arrived, Manstein also had the 62nd and 294th Infantry Divisions plus *Luftwaffe* ground forces equivalent to a third division, as well as an Alpine division. Other units dribbled in. The 57th Panzer Corps, for instance, was sent from Army Group A, but it was slow getting away because an unseasonal thaw suddenly set in and many of the supply lorries got stuck.

Planning the rescue attempt

While his forces were gathering, Manstein set about studying the maps and deciding on how best to go about breaking through to Stalingrad. He divided his forces into two. On his left, or west, around Rychkov he gathered what became known as Army Detachment Hollidt, commanded by General Karl-Adolf Hollidt of the 17th Corps. To the right, or the east, was the 4th Panzer Army under Hoth. Both groups would be continually reinforced in preparation for the campaign to come.

Manstein knew that Hollidt was closer to Stalingrad than Hoth – he was only 40 kilometres (25 miles or so) away – but he chose not to attack here. Hollidt had a long and insecurely held left flank that ran for miles along the Chir River to link up with the Hungarian 2nd Army. Soviet forces were known to be lurking along this flank and Manstein worried that if Hollidt put most of his strength into an attack the Soviets would punch through this weak flank. Not only that, but the short distance to Stalingrad made this the obvious place to attack and Manstein guessed, correctly, that most of the Soviet strength would be placed there to stop the move. Manstein therefore decided to instruct Hollidt to make a series of small-scale attacks, as if probing the Soviet defences in preparation for a major offensive. This, Manstein hoped, would draw the Soviets' attention and reserves to Rychkov.

Meanwhile, the real blow would be delivered by Hoth. Hoth too had a vulnerable flank – this time his right flank, which ran along the edge of the Kalmyk Steppe. There had been no obvious Soviet activity here, but to make sure Hoth sent out a three-day patrol, carried out by fast-moving motorcycle troops backed up by light tanks. Apart from a few Russian cavalry scouts they found nothing. The flanks seemed safe.

Dealing with the second element, making the trapped 6th Army ready for its escape, gave Manstein just as much trouble. Manstein knew that if the break-out was to work, the trapped 6th Army would need to attack towards the relieving force, while being prepared to move quickly and efficiently out of the trap. But being prepared to move out was not necessarily the same deployment as that needed for a robust defence. Moreover, Manstein hesitated to tell Paulus in which direction he should break out in case the Soviets got to hear of it and guessed Manstein's plan.

The movement of the 6th Army was to be crucial, for it was by far the largest and most powerful element in Manstein's Army Group Don. Trapped in the Stalingrad pocket were thirteen German infantry divisions, three panzer divisions, three panzergrenadier divisions, one anti-aircraft division, two Romanian divisions, one Croat regiment and a number of engineering units. There were also the headquarters staffs for all these units, plus that of the 6th Army itself. In all there were some 220,000 German frontline troops, 15,000 German support troops and staff and about 10,000 allies. It was a large and formidable military force, but it was short on supplies of all kinds.

A key problem shared by Manstein and Paulus was communication. There was only an intermittent direct radio link between the two men, so all communications went via the OKH, which meant that Hitler got to see and interfere with all messages. Alternatively, an officer could fly to Stalingrad and back with written or verbal messages. It was far from ideal. What made it worse was that Hitler was sending messages and instructions to Paulus without sending copies to Manstein. These messages were usually strong on exhortations to hold out and stand firm, but short on detail of how Paulus was to do this.

Paulus's failure to break out

Moreover, Paulus was fully aware that any break-out attempt would result in heavy casualties for the 6th Army. And he knew that those casualties would fall disproportionately on the infantry and even more so on those forming the rearguard of the dash to join Manstein. Even the most optimistic estimates reckoned that the rear 15 per cent of the army would suffer 100 per cent casualties. By contrast, the 6th Army was relatively safe where it was, dug into strong defensive positions. If it could hold out until the spring, when the Russians would lose the advantage they always had in winter fighting, the bulk of the 6th Army would be able to get out intact. But that would depend on the amount of supplies that the *Luftwaffe* could fly in.

It is impossible to deduce from the messages and diaries that survive exactly what Paulus's intentions were in early December. All we do know is that he constantly raised problems and objections whenever Manstein contacted him about the break-out.

The behaviour of the third element, the Soviet army, was making it clear to Manstein that if a break-out was going to happen it had to happen sooner rather than later. Hollidt was coming under increasingly frequent attack. Although none of these Soviet assaults was particularly strong, and Manstein guessed that they were intended merely to disrupt Hollidt's assault forces, they were strong enough to be a worry. If the Russians were preparing a major attack, Hollidt and his units might not be able to hold the line. Already the 11th Panzer Division had only half of its tanks ready for battle – the rest were being repaired or serviced, or had been lost to enemy fire.

Manstein gave orders that his offensive, codenamed 'Winter Storm', would begin on 12 December. He gave Hoth his orders, and told Paulus to be ready to break out within 48 hours. Hoth launched his panzers forward at dawn, after a whirlwind artillery barrage. Behind them came a mass of lorries, tractors pulling trailers and other vehicles, all carrying a mass of supplies for the beleaguered 6th Army. Their task, once having delivered their loads, was to pick up the wounded and sick and carry them back out again.

The Russian defence was relatively light. It consisted only of the 51st Army, a largely infantry force which had been reduced in strength only a week earlier when Zhukov had stripped it of heavy weapons for use against the 6th Army. Hoth advanced almost 48 kilometres (30 miles) on that first day. After that he successfully maintained the momentum of the advance, though the daily march was soon down to 16 kilometres (10 miles). On 17 December his lead units reached the Aksai River. They found the 21-metre-wide (70 feet) river frozen over, but not solid enough to carry the weight of a tank. The panzers had to use bridges, and there were only two in existence. The arrival of the 17th Panzer Division in the front line that day tipped the balance and by dusk Hoth was over the river in strength.

Now was the time for Paulus to break out of Stalingrad, using his panzers to lead the way. He would then hurry south to meet Hoth. But he did not do it. On 18 December, Manstein sent his chief intelligence officer and trusted subordinate, Major Hans Eismann, into Stalingrad by air to talk to Paulus. As with the meetings on 24 November, all of the participants in the meeting that followed later give different versions of who said what to whom, no doubt in an effort to evade responsibility for what followed. It is, however, possible to work out the main outline of what occurred.

Present at the meeting were Eismann, Paulus and General Arthur Schmidt, the 6th Army chief of staff, plus a number of other staff officers. It seems the meeting began with Eismann giving his hosts a briefing on the progress of Operation Winter Storm. He then passed on Manstein's order that Operation Thunderclap (the break-out by the 6th Army) had to take place at once. Paulus acknowledged that a break-out was necessary, but was unsure whether this was the correct moment. He then called on his various heads of department – supply, artillery, and so on – to give their opinions. They all later claimed that they had advocated an immediate break-out, and blamed the others for not agreeing.

Finally Paulus turned to Schmidt. Everyone agreed that it was Schmidt who asserted that it was impossible to break out within 48 hours, as Manstein demanded. Schmidt finished by banging the table and declaring, 'The 6th Army can hold out until Easter if it has to. All you lot have to do is keep us supplied.' Paulus nodded and said he agreed. He told Eismann that the 6th Army could not move.

It was early on 19 December before Eismann got back to Manstein. He arrived just as news came in that

Hoth's leading panzers had reached the Mishkova River. This was the last big natural obstacle to be overcome on the way to Stalingrad, and it was lined with large numbers of Russian defenders.

Hoth reported that he was doubtful of his ability to fight his way over the Mishkova unless the Russian defenders were assaulted from the rear by Paulus and his panzers. Manstein sent an urgent message to Zeitzler at the OKH insisting that 'this is the last possible moment for a break-out as a means of preserving the bulk of the troops of the 6th Army'. There was no reply. The hours ticked by.

No news came from Hitler or from Zeitzler. At 6 pm Manstein heard that the intermittent radio link to Paulus was working. He sent Paulus a direct order: '6th Army attack will begin at once'. There was an acknowledgement, but no reply.

Next morning Paulus replied that he could not move because he did not have enough fuel. But by then it was too late. Manstein, who had other problems, had told Hoth to pull back.

The trap closes further

On 16 December a large Soviet attack had been launched across the Don some miles to the west, where the Italian 8th Army, under Weichs and Army Group B, held the line. The Italians fought well while their ammunition lasted, but fled at sunset, after which the Russians surged through a gap 48 kilometres wide (30 miles). The 27th Panzer Division led a counterattack, but within 48 hours it had been effectively destroyed. This offensive was not so dangerous as it had at first appeared. The Soviets abandoned their version of the Germans' blitzkrieg tactics and instead reverted to their old method of advancing on a broad front with tanks and artillery mixed up with the infantry.

Weichs asked Manstein to take over the eastern end of the gap and launch a counterattack. Manstein, however, had no reserves to hand since all of his spare units were supporting Hoth. Balck led his 11th Panzer Division into the eastern flank of the advancing Russians and brought them to a halt, but elsewhere the Soviets pushed on. It was this news that convinced Manstein that he had to pull Hoth back. If Paulus had been moving, Manstein claims, Hoth would have been ordered to stay put to ensure the safety of the 6th Army, but with Paulus staying put, Manstein ordered the retreat.

At 5.20 am on 24 December, Soviet tanks burst out of the darkness to attack the airfield at Tatsinskaya. This was the busiest of the airfields from which the *Luftwaffe* was supplying the 6th Army. Of the 196 transport aircraft on the ground when the Soviets attacked, 72 were destroyed. This represented about 20 per cent of the aircraft being used to supply Paulus. Although the Russians were driven off and the airfield recaptured, the incident had not only reduced the capacity of the *Luftwaffe* to supply the trapped men – it had also shown how precarious that supply route really was.

General Schmidt's boast that the 6th Army would still be fighting at Easter was starting to look increasingly unlikely.

12
THE HUNGRY BATTLE

The defeat of Operation Winter Storm had been a severe blow to the German army, though not everyone at the time recognized just how serious the failure to break through had been. Inside Stalingrad, Paulus and Schmidt continued to talk about holding out until the spring. In the Caucasus, Kleist maintained his positions. At his command headquarters, Hitler showed no particular signs of distress. Only Manstein seems to have understood that the 6th Army was finished and that the whole of Army Group A was in the greatest danger.

Conserving supplies

The future of the men in Stalingrad depended almost entirely on the ability of the *Luftwaffe* to keep them supplied. Even at the start of the encirclement that ability had been in doubt, but now maintaining supplies was proving impossible. Inside the defensive perimeter there were three airfields. The largest was that at Pitomnik, with Gumrak only slightly smaller. The third field, at Stalingradsky, was much smaller and of little use to large transport aircraft such as the Junkers Ju52 or converted Heinkel He111 bombers. Outside the isolated pocket the main base was at Tatsinskaya, but after that airfield had been badly damaged by the Russians on 24 December supply aircraft had to come in from further afield. Salsk was used first, but by mid-January the Soviets were too close for comfort and the *Luftwaffe* moved to Zverevo.

The shortest route was from Tatsinskaya to Pitomnik, a flying time of about one hour and 40 minutes. Given the time taken to load and unload the aircraft, that meant that each Ju52 could make only one round trip each day. It was very soon obvious that this was not enough.

It was rare that the *Luftwaffe* could fly in 150 tons of supplies in a day, far short of what was needed. The most successful day was 19 December when 289 tons of supplies were flown in, but the total soon dropped and by early January the *Luftwaffe* was averaging just under 100 tons per day.

It was not as if the *Luftwaffe* did not try. The pilots and the aircrew were deeply shocked by the conditions that they saw inside the pocket as the siege dragged on, and particularly by the emaciated condition of the soldiers. They did their utmost to fly supplies in and take the wounded out. Indeed, some 42,000 men were evacuated from Stalingrad by air, the vast majority of them wounded soldiers, though the German high command insisted that some specialist technicians and officers were brought out as well.

The Russians made great efforts to stop the air bridge to the 6th Army. Fighters patrolled the skies and anti-aircraft guns ringed the pocket. Soviet aircraft also attacked the airfields, destroying stores after they had been landed and pockmarking the landing strips with craters to make using the airfields increasingly hazardous. The losses suffered by the *Luftwaffe* were high. In all 266 Junkers Ju52s, 165 Heinkel He111s, 42 Junkers Ju86s and 9 Fw 200 Condors were destroyed. Perhaps even more serious was the loss of over 850 aircrew.

Paulus had to make some tough decisions about supplies. His first was one of the easiest: the panzers were refused permission to move. Each tank had to be parked amid the ruins or dug into an emplacement from where it could use its gun as an artillery weapon. The few reserves of fuel that existed were hoarded, to be used only when a major Russian offensive began, because that would be the time when the panzers would need to be able to move.

Ammunition was likewise severely restricted. Each man was given only 15 or 20 rounds of ammunition each day. The troops were ordered to open fire only when they had a good target and a reasonable prospect of hitting it. The reserves of small arms ammunition were held back at regimental and divisional level to ensure that they were not frittered away in daily use but were kept ready for when the Soviets launched a real attack. The artillery was similarly kept short. Previously the big guns had fired frequently and often, but now they lay quiet for hours on end. Sometimes entire days went by without any fighting taking place at all. The men just huddled in their trenches and froze.

Food supplies were the most difficult of all. The horses were killed after the failure of Operation Winter Storm, as their fodder had run out and there was no future use for them. The horsemeat was eaten up quickly, and then there was no more. By 20 December the combination of a lack of food, the intense cold and the enormous stress of the situation caused the outbreak of a strange new phenomenon. Men would look perfectly well when seen by their comrades, but an hour later they would be found dead without a mark on them. They might be on sentry duty or sleeping in a dugout, but the mysterious death caught up with them all the same. The causes of the deaths were hotly debated at the time, but it now seems likely there was no single reason, rather a combination of all the different factors.

Hunger came to dominate conversations, thoughts and dreams. Everyone was short of food, some were quite literally starving to death. Back at headquarters, Zeitzler the logistics expert was so concerned that he put himself on a diet with a similar calorie count to that of the men in Stalingrad. In a few weeks he lost 12.7 kilograms (two stone) even though his lifestyle was much less demanding than that of the men in the doomed city. Hitler was alarmed by his gaunt appearance and ordered him to eat more food, putting a guard on him at meal times to ensure that he did so.

Disease and illness

Diseases broke out in epidemic form, further weakening some of the soldiers and reducing the number available for fighting. Hepatitis struck early on, bringing with it a loss of appetite and increased lethargy. Dysentery, that old enemy of armies in the field, came in mid-December and never left. Although the German doctors understood the causes and the treatment of dysentery, it was difficult to cure the disease in the conditions that prevailed in Stalingrad and impossible to eradicate it. By early January typhus was spreading through the 6th Army, killing around 15 per cent of those who caught it.

That typhus was spread by lice was well understood at the time, and had been for over half a century, but the conditions in Stalingrad were not conducive to getting rid of them. Head lice can be eliminated by diligent combing with a narrow-toothed comb, or by shaving the head. Body lice are more difficult to deal with, because they live not only on the body and on body hair but also in clothing. To get rid of body lice it is necessary to wash all clothing and bedding at around 55 degrees Celsius (131 degrees Fahrenheit), or leave the items unworn or unused for seven days or more. In the unhygienic conditions of the trenches and dugouts this was impossible. Even if clothes could have been washed at high temperatures, the cramped conditions meant that re-infection by comrades would have taken place fairly quickly.

Frostbite was also becoming an increasingly common problem. There were no new supplies of clothing coming into Stalingrad, so the men had to make do with what they had. Socks and boots wore out first, so the number of cases of frostbite of the foot increased rapidly. Not only did the incidence of frostbite increase, so did its severity. Men had previously been out of action for a few days, but now they were laid up for weeks and death was no longer rare.

Great diligence and effort is required to keep an army in the field healthy. Inside Stalingrad neither the tools nor the time were available, so men fell sick and died with increasing frequency and speed. By 3 January Paulus calculated that of the 150,000 men in Stalingrad only about 35,000 were fit for duty.

If supplies in general were low, and getting lower,

one flow from the outside actually speeded up. Promotions and awards of medals and decorations began to be made with greater rapidity and, a dispassionate observer might think, less justification than had been the case before the 6th Army was surrounded. Paulus himself was promoted to Generalleutnant, one grade above the usual rank for the commander of an infantry army, and he was awarded the prestigious Oak Leaves to add to the Knight's Cross that he already held. Officers and other ranks all received decorations of various kinds.

In fact the promotions and decorations were all part of a carefully crafted propaganda campaign designed by Josef Goebbels. It was now obvious that a disaster of epic proportions was unfolding at Stalingrad, and despite the blackout on news rumours were sweeping the army and beginning to filter back home. Sooner or later the tragic events would have to be revealed. It was Goebbels' job to ensure that German morale, both at home and among fighting men, did not suffer too much as a result.

A legion of heroes

In order to cope with the disaster, Goebbels completely changed the image of Nazi Germany and his entire propaganda campaign. Up until New Year 1943 Goebbels and his minions had portrayed Nazi Germany as the harbinger of a New Order for Europe, a new social, political and economic system that would sweep away the decadent, failed and discredited wreckage of the Old Europe that had perished in the Great War of 1914–18. Nazism had been portrayed as youthful, vibrant, dynamic and irresistible. But now all that had changed.

The 6th Army was hailed as being a legion of heroes worthy of the finest traditions of the ancient Teutonic warriors. The spirit of Arminius, who had ousted the Romans from Germany, was invoked, along with that of Frederick the Great, Emperor Frederick Barbarossa, Blücher and many more. This was the reason behind the promotions and the awards. The 6th Army had to be built up to be the finest that Germany had ever fielded. In truth it was good, but it had never been as good as Goebbels now claimed.

The message that Goebbels was slowly and carefully crafting was that the 6th Army was heroically sacrificing itself to save the ancient civilization of Europe from the onslaught of the barbaric Asiatic hordes pouring out of Siberia. As the end approached, Goebbels ensured that radio broadcasts, newspaper reports and speeches by Nazi leaders were peppered with allusions to ancient German legends and myths. Most frequently, references were made to the *Nibelungenlied*, an epic poem which ends with a heroic German wreaking terrible but suicidal revenge on King Etzel of the Huns by setting fire to the royal palace. The similarity to the suicidal stand of the 6th Army against the Russians was clear. Goebbels made Nazi Germany the self-appointed heir to Athens, Rome, Christianity and two thousand years of European civilization. It was to become the mainstay of German propaganda for the rest of the war.

Back in Stalingrad, Paulus received a New Year

message from the Führer, that he was instructed to pass on to his men.

'In the name of the whole German people, I send you and your valiant army the heartiest good wishes for the New Year. The hardness of your perilous position is known to me. The heroic stand of your troops has my highest respect. You and your soldiers, however, should enter the New Year with the unshakeable confidence that I and the whole German armed forces will do everything in our power to relieve the defenders of Stalingrad and that with your staunchness will come the most glorious feat ever in the history of German arms.'

'Adolf Hitler'

Paulus sent a reply, also read out to his men.

'Mein Führer.'

'Your confident words were greeted here with great enthusiasm. We will justify your trust. You

can be certain that we – from the oldest general to the youngest grenadier – will hold out inspired with a fanatical will and contribute our share to the final victory. Our will for victory is unbroken, and the New Year will bring our release. When this will be I cannot yet say. The Führer has never gone back on his word and this time will be no different.'

'Paulus'

It was all nonsense aimed at keeping up morale. In a private message sent to Hitler, Paulus confessed what was really going on. 'My army is starving to death.'

Army Group A falls back

While the 6th Army slowly died, arguments raged in the German high command about what should be done about Army Group A down in the Caucasus. Weichs, Manstein and Kleist, the commanders on the spot, were all of the opinion that the forces were dangerously exposed and had to be withdrawn. Back at the OKH, Ziegler was equally worried about their supply situation, while Hitler was already looking forward to the summer campaign of 1943.

Hitler had not yet decided what to do that summer, but he was insistent on one point. Army Group A must not be withdrawn completely. It had to maintain a toehold south of Rostov from which a new offensive could be launched at some future date. The idea was a sensible one. Even if no such attack was ever delivered, the mere presence of men south of Rostov would keep the Russians guessing as to the Germans' intentions and force them to keep forces in the Caucasus.

The situation was complicated by disputes over the command structure. The area had originally been under the control of a single military command, Army Group South. In spring 1942 that had been divided into Army Group A and Army Group B. There was now a third unit, Army Group Don. This was clearly one too many, and if the men were withdrawn from the Caucasus it might be two too many.

Neither Weichs, Kleist nor Manstein wanted to lose their command, so each put forward a plan for the withdrawal that involved one of the other army groups being disbanded.

In the event the issue was forced when the Russians launched three simultaneous offensives in the first week of January. The first two were launched in the Caucasus and achieved little, but the third erupted out of the Kalmyk Steppe and captured Elista, the base from which the Germans had been patrolling that vast area. The Russians surged on and at one point their advanced scouting units got within 112 kilometres (70 miles) of Rostov. Even Hitler had to admit that it was time to retreat.

Kleist calculated that the railway lines through Rostov were going to be fully used when transporting the 1st Panzer Army with its tanks, halftracks and huge number of lorries. The 17th Army was therefore ordered to march west down the Kuban River to reach the Kuban Peninsula that projected out into the Black Sea towards the Kerch Peninsula of the Crimea. There they were to dig in, to form Hitler's toehold in the area. By holding on to the naval base of Novorossiysk they would also keep the activities of the Soviet Black Sea Fleet severely curtailed.

By 10 January, Kleist was holding a rearguard line along the Kuma River. His left flank was falling back in front of a renewed Soviet thrust from Elista and the Kalmyk Steppe. Kleist asked Manstein for help in fending off this assault, more than 160 kilometres (100 miles) behind his front lines. Manstein sent what few units he could spare, but his attention was by this date fixed on his own front. The Russians were on the move at Stalingrad.

Paulus surrenders

At dawn on 9 January the Russian guns fell silent. Then two Soviet officers, accompanied by a bugler carrying a large white flag, appeared in front of the German lines near Marinovka at the far western end of the pocket. 'We are envoys from the commander of the Red Army,' shouted out one officer in good German. 'We have a message for your commander-in-chief.' There was a delay while the sergeant in charge of that section of the German trenches went off to fetch his officer. When the officer arrived he agreed to take the Russians to Paulus, but on condition that they were blindfolded.

The Russian officers allowed themselves to be blindfolded, then were led past the German lines to the German regimental headquarters. While the Russians sat waiting, a radio message was sent to the headquarters of the 6th Army. The German colonel received a reply and told the Russians that a staff car was being sent for them. He asked the Russians what their message was. He was shown a sealed packet, but the Russians denied any knowledge of what was in it.

In fact the message was a demand from the Soviet commander General Konstantin Rokossovsky, for the surrender of the 6th Army. The opening paragraph read:

'Herr General Paulus,
'All hopes for the rescue of your troops by a German
offensive from the south and southwest have fallen

through. The German troops which hastened to your assistance have been routed. The German transport planes that supplied you with miserable quantities of food, ammunition and fuel are frequently compelled to change their aerodromes and cover long distances to reach the positions of your surrounded troops. They suffer tremendous losses in aircraft and crews. The position of your encircled troops is desperate. They are experiencing hunger, disease and cold. The bitter frost, the cold biting winds and the snowstorms have yet to come. Your men have not been supplied with winter uniforms, and live in appalling unhygienic conditions. You as the commander must realize full well that you have no real chance of breaking out of the ring of encirclement. Your situation is hopeless and further resistance is useless.'

The message went on to ask for an immediate surrender. In return, Rokossovsky offered good rations, comfortable living accommodation and treatment according to international conventions. If surrender was not immediate, however, no promises were made about good treatment or the lives of German troops. It was a grim message.

When the staff car arrived from Paulus it carried a staff colonel, who entered and saluted. He told the Russians that he was under strict orders not to take anything from them, nor to listen to any verbal message and was to do nothing except escort them back to the Russian positions in safety. The Russians tried to give him the sealed package, but he refused, so they donned their blindfolds and were led back into no man's land.

At 6 am on the following morning 7,000 Russian guns opened fire on the German positions on the western side of the Stalingrad pocket, and kept on firing for an hour. When the guns fell silent, the Soviet infantry swarmed forward, supported by T34 tanks. The offensive was being carried out by the 21st and 65th Armies and was intended by Rokossovsky to crush the 6th Army completely. His intelligence reports told him that there were only 85,000 men in the pocket, most of whom were unfit for duty, and that the Germans had virtually no ammunition or fuel left.

As a consequence the Russians did not expect to meet much in the way of resistance. They reverted to the tactics that had served them so badly in the first months of the war. They had been given orders that 'If the Fascists do not surrender they must die'. Many Russians took this to mean that since the 6th Army had not surrendered then all of the enemy must be shot. Many prisoners were shot down in rear areas, and at one field hospital all of the wounded and sick were machine-gunned, while the medical staff were taken off to work at a Soviet hospital.

On the first day of the attack the Russians succeeded in breaking through the German front lines. They overran the Romanians waiting in reserve and pushed on towards Stalingrad. News of this breakthrough had reached Manstein at the same time that Kleist had asked him for help. Manstein was worried that if Stalingrad fell, the full might of the Russian armies would pour south to attack him within days.

But on the second day of the Russian attack, Paulus recognized that this was the main Russian assault to destroy the 6th Army. He released both fuel and ammunition to the 16th Panzer Division. When the panzers went into action they gave the Soviets a severe shock, allowing other German and Romanian units to rally, reform and rejoin the battle. By dusk on 12 January the Soviet 'final offensive' had ground to a halt on the banks of the Rossoshka River. They had lost over 30,000 men and half of their tanks.

The Germans had won a reprieve, but it could only be temporary. Hitler ordered the *Luftwaffe* to make renewed efforts to get supplies through. He sent more aircraft and aircrew, but it would take time for them to arrive and the 6th Army was running out of time.

On 16 January Rokossovsky launched another attack. The Russians crossed the Rossoshka and later that day they captured the large airfield at Pitomnik. Supplies could now reach the beleaguered 6th Army only through Gumrak, and that airfield was so badly battered that most *Luftwaffe* pilots chose to parachute supplies down rather than land. That meant that the wounded could no longer get out. Medical officers now stopped treating the mortally wounded and instead concentrated their efforts and drugs on men who had a chance of recovery. When soldiers carried in the badly wounded they were advised to shoot them to spare their suffering.

The new Russian advance ended on 17 January, having taken half of the area of the pocket. That day Paulus issued orders to his men to break out. His plan was that the men who were fit to fight should punch a hole in the Soviet lines to the south of the pocket. The men would then scatter into the open steppe and try to find their way through to the German lines. Some soldiers got hold of Russian overcoats from enemy bodies to aid the attempt. The orders for the attack were never given, but some officers and men did slip through the Soviet lines. They were found over the following weeks out on the frozen steppes. None got to safety.

The end was by now clearly in sight. On 20 January

Paulus wrote a farewell note to his wife, put it in a packet with his signet ring and then slipped it into a parcel of official despatches to be taken out by one of the few couriers. Orders arrived from Hitler that one man from each division had to be flown out. Paulus could not think why, but Hitler had plans of his own. More understandable to Paulus was the order to use experienced panzer officers as couriers – their skills would obviously be much in demand in the campaigns to come.

One of the last senior officers to fly out was General Hans-Valentin Hube, commander of the 14th Panzer Corps. Hitler rated Hube highly and referred to him as 'Hube, the Man'. He had ordered Hube's evacuation on 18 January, but Hube refused until he was forced on to an aircraft two days later.

On 22 January, Gumrak airfield fell to the Russians. There was now only the small airfield at Stalingradsky, accessible only to small aircraft. Supplies could come in only by parachute.

By 24 January the Germans had been pushed back

into the ruined city. Two days later Soviet tanks from the attacking units broke through to reach Chuikov's 62nd Army. The Germans were now broken into two pockets.

Paulus was in the southern pocket, where he received a radio message from Hitler.

> 'Surrender is out of the question. Troops must fight to the end. If possible, hold a reduced Fortress with those troops still battleworthy. Bravery and tenacity of Fortress have provided the opportunity to establish a new front and launch counterattacks. The 6th Army has fulfilled its historic contribution in the greatest passage in German history.'

The reaction of Paulus to the message is not recorded. Hitler was right about one thing – the new front had been established. Kleist had got the last of his units back across the Don at Rostov and the 17th Army was well dug in at Kuban. It had been a close-run thing, but Kleist had managed to get all of his men and their equipment away from a possible encirclement, beside which the disaster of Stalingrad would have seemed petty. Kleist was promoted to the rank of field marshal for his achievements.

He was not the only general to be raised to this exalted rank. On 30 January Hitler also made Paulus a field marshal. When he received news of his promotion, Paulus was prostrate on his bed with dysentery. His army was collapsing as entire units surrendered or were wiped out. Paulus will have known as well as Hitler that no German field marshal had ever surrendered to an enemy. Whether Hitler intended Paulus to continue fighting or commit suicide is unclear. But Paulus chose neither.

The next day Russian lieutenant Fedor Yelchenko was about to lead an assault on the ruins of a large shop in Stalingrad's central square when, according to the interview he gave a week later:

'Suddenly up popped a German officer carrying a white flag and accompanied by an interpreter. I

shouted out, asking what he wanted. He asked for a senior officer to meet his senior officer. I said, "I am the nearest thing to a senior officer here right now. What does your officer want?" The German said that his officer wanted to surrender. "Very good," I replied.

'I led two of my men into the ruined store. It was alive with Germans, hundreds of them. They all had guns. My men were nervous. The German officer led us down into the cellar and introduced us to Colonel Rasske. This Rasske behaved like a real officer without any fear or arrogance. He introduced me to General Schmidt, who said Field Marshal Paulus was too ill to talk to me. Rasske was commanding the men in the store. Rasske and Schmidt kept going to talk to a man lying on a bed. This was Paulus. He did not look very ill, but sort of unhappy. Rasske asked me the terms of surrender. What could I say? I was a lieutenant. I said that General Rokossovsky had issued an ultimatum and that those were the terms.

'Then Rasske asked me if I had any questions for

Paulus. I said "No" because the position was very clear to me. Rasske then asked me to prevent Paulus from being manhandled or treated like a tramp. I asked if he was surrendering the store to me. Rasske said he was. Then I went and signalled to HQ. They sent a good car and a large guard to collect Paulus. I took away his little pistol from him before he was driven off. I left him his pen-knife as he said he needed it.'

Paulus was questioned by Rokossovsky and he confirmed that he was surrendering the entire southern pocket of troops. He agreed to send an order to the men in the northern pocket to surrender, but it was two days before they did and a few isolated outposts held out for a further two days.

The Battle of Stalingrad was over. The Germans had lost.

13
THE BEGINNING OF THE END

It is almost impossible to overestimate the importance of the German disaster at Stalingrad. In the campaign as a whole the Wehrmacht had lost perhaps 15 per cent of its strength, but had gained almost nothing.

Coming to terms with failure

Despite Goebbels' best efforts, the scale of the disaster could not be hidden. It has been said, with some justification, that every civilian in Germany knew a family who had lost a son at Stalingrad. The sense of shock in Germany was great, but the blow to the morale of the soldiers was greater. Ever since the invasion of Russia had begun they had known nothing but victory, even if those battlefield successes had not translated into final victory. Now they had suffered a battlefield defeat, and one of massive proportions. The self-belief of the German soldiers had been badly dented and in many cases destroyed. They no longer viewed the Russians as poor soldiers to be defeated, but as tough opponents of whom it paid to be wary.

On 18 February 1943, Goebbels delivered his famous Sportpalast speech, so named because it was delivered to a large invited audience at the Berlin Sportpalast. This was the first speech in which any Nazi leader admitted that the war was proceeding anything other than smoothly for Germany. He outlined the setbacks on the Eastern Front, explained that the whole future of European civilization was at threat from a Communist takeover and stated that only Germany could save Europe. He reached a climax by asking his audience, and via radio the entire German people,

'Do you believe with the Führer and us in the final total victory of the German people? Are you and the German people willing to work, if the Führer orders, 10, 12 and if necessary 14 hours a day and to give everything for victory? Do you want total war? If necessary, do you want a war more total and radical than anything that we can even imagine today?'

The response was overwhelmingly positive. Germany was put on a war footing for the first time. The production of consumer goods ended and factories were turned over to manufacturing war *matériel* on a massive scale. Slave labour from conquered countries was still used, but German workers were increasingly pushed to work longer and harder. Greater and greater sacrifices were called for in terms of effort, money and lives. For many Germans, Stalingrad represented a crucial turning point in the war.

In addition to this loss suffered by the Germans, there had been gains by the Red Army. The Soviet forces had grown larger with each month, as an increasing number of men were called up and more and more resources were poured into the manufacture of weapons. The success of Operation Uranus showed that the Russians were able to mimic German blitzkrieg tactics when the right men were in command and they had appropriate equipment. This was not always the case, and in the coming months the Russians would regularly fall back on their old tactics, with often fatal results. But the improvement in the Russian forces could not be denied.

There would be much fighting and bloodshed to come on the Eastern Front, but after Stalingrad there was no longer any chance that the Germans could win an outright, total victory over the Soviet Union. There was talk among the senior military commanders of opening negotiations with the Russians to agree a peace deal. Hitler refused point blank. Unlike many of the military men, Hitler was fully aware of the mass murders, genocide and other war crimes that the SS and other instruments of the Nazi Party had been carrying out in occupied Russia. He knew that the Russians were intent on vengeance and that talks were pointless. Later the sure knowledge that he himself would be executed would lead Hitler to prolong the war needlessly and finally to take his own life.

Stalingrad marked the beginning of the end for the Third Reich.

The cost of victory and defeat

The human cost of the Stalingrad campaign was immense. Among the greatest suffering was that endured by the civilian population of the city. On 23 August 1942 the city of Stalingrad had a population of 400,000 civilians. The fate of most of these people is quite unknown. Many fled, others joined the Red Army, but the majority were trapped in the city by the German advance and the refusal of the NKVD to allow civilians to use the ferries to cross the river. In 1943, after the battle, the NKVD counted the civilians still living in the city. The statistics from the three central areas make for depressing reading. Traktorozavodskiy District had been home to a population of 75,000 in 1942, but by 1943 there were only 150 people alive. In Barrikadniy District 76 people remained out of 50,000 and in Ermanskiy District 32 out of 45,000 had survived. It is thought that around 200,000 civilians were killed during the fighting.

The casualties suffered by the Red Army were just as horrific. Most accounts state that of the 10,000 men of the 13th Rifles that crossed the Volga into the Battle of Stalingrad, only between 280 and 320 survived the struggle. Several regiments and battalions were entirely wiped out. The official returns of the Red Army list 478,741 men killed and 650,878 wounded in and around the city, but this is generally thought to be an underestimation. The figures do not include the campaigns fought outside the city. The Soviets may have lost as many as 650,000 dead.

Not all of the Soviet casualties were caused by the Germans. The NKVD records show that they executed 13,541 men and women, both soldiers and civilians, during the Battle of Stalingrad. That is, they shot them after a trial, however brief. The numbers of troops shot dead by enforcement squads when they were seen to retreat, or did not attack with sufficient vigour, was never recorded.

The recovery of Stalingrad took a long time. The following is an account written by S. Sorokin, a factory foreman brought in to help rebuild the Red October Factory after the fighting ended.

'We reached train station Archeda and went further on foot. It was very cold. We walked for two days. Spent the night in desolate dugouts. We arrived in the city on February 14. At the territory

of the plant we met the director P. A. Matevosyan, and the director of the garage V. J. Jukov. They arrived at the plant first and took over from the military commander. They notified us: all areas of the plant are a solid minefield. It is possible only to go on trails made by sappers. We began to search for a place for housing for ourselves. We decided to set up temporary housing directly on the factory premises. We walked into open-hearth plant N1. It was necessary to examine a basement location. We looked around quietly and came to a hole in the wall of the shop. Suddenly we saw a machine-gun positioned in a hole in a wall, aiming at a checkpoint. We had no weapons ourselves. What to do? Should we go further into the shop or not? We stayed; it was necessary to look around further. We heard steps from the direction of the Volga. Two Fascist soldiers with mess-tins came nearer to our shop. They made a bee-line for the machine-gun. Upon seeing us, they were dumbfounded. After some *confusion they began to jabber on in bad Russian language: "We work kitchen and garage." But we knew there was no functioning kitchen or garage on the territory of the plant any longer. We said "ok" and passed by. After some minutes we met a young soldier – a submachine-gunner, and asked him: "Have you collected all prisoners of war in the territory of the plant?" "Yes, of course," he answered. "More than one week ago. What happened?" "We saw two Fascists and a machine-gun position," we answered. "Hm... Go" he said. He went into the shop with us behind him. We went down into a cellar. We went on in full darkness. We passed one basement location, and another. In the third was visible a wooden desktop, oven, mess-tins, a wick lamp. On cots the Germans puttered about. Our soldier lit the cellar by flash-light and shouted: "Weapons on desktop." The Fascist soldiers rose from their cots, and put their pistols and other weapons on the desk. The soldier led them to headquarters.'*

In March a British reporter based in Moscow was flown to Stalingrad by the Soviets to view the ruined city. He sent back several detailed reports about what his escorts told him and showed him, then added a short piece about something he found himself.

'I remember it was just about the time I began to look at the ground as I walked along. When you are sick of a sight, you look at the ground and that way it seems a quicker journey. I was sick of looking at the savaged ruins of Stalingrad, sick of registering shock after shock of the power and terror and pity. The power of blast, the terror of the shapelessness of common things, the pity of scraps of household intimacies.

'It was just about then that I noticed a stick standing upright in the rubble. It had a cardboard notice on it which said, very firmly and boldly, "Hole No.37". Just then a woman's head appeared beside the little stick. Behind her came two children, one a girl of three all muffled up in a white woolly cap with flaps like rabbit's ears, another little girl dark and solemn about five. The woman went towards some washing that hung on a line, frozen stiff and flapping in the bitter wind like three-ply boards in a gale. The little girls ran up towards a toy sledge.

'I stopped and talked to the woman. She answered in monosyllables, and her voice had that tone that women put on when they talk of the idiocy of men. Yes, she had been there all the time. It was terrible. Yes, it was very difficult to live. Her husband was in the army, she had to keep her children with her because there had been no time to send them away.

'Why did she stay? Why did she live for five months in a hole in the ground between two armies and why was it postmarked "Hole No.37"? Her answer was very feminine. She was doing washing for the Red Army.

'I turned to the Red Army major who was escorting me around. "How many other such holes are there in Stalingrad?" I asked. He shrugged his shoulders. There were many he said, but he did not know how many.'

The German losses proved to be crippling to their war effort. It is estimated that a total of 750,000 personnel were killed, wounded or taken prisoner. These figures include Romanian and Italian losses. There has been much controversy over exactly how many men were trapped in the pocket around Stalingrad. The official figures reported by Paulus on 6 December show that 275,000 daily rations were needed by the 6th Army. Not all of these rations were given out to German soldiers. There were 12,600 Romanians and 500 Italians as well. There were also 20,300 Russians in German employment. Nobody is certain how accurate these figures were. In the confusion of the retreat into Stalingrad many units got broken up and disorganized. No doubt many commanders sent in an estimate, and most would have put forward a higher figure in an effort to get more food. There may, in fact, have been as few as 220,000 men trapped in the pocket.

However many men were trapped, it is certain that around 42,000 were flown out for one reason or another. The Soviets captured 111,465 men, of whom 91,000 surrendered right at the end. The rest of the trapped men must have been killed. The Soviets treated their prisoners very badly and before the spring came half of them had died from disease, starvation and execution. In the summer of 1943 the survivors became slave labour. They were put to work rebuilding Stalingrad or were sent to farms or factories elsewhere. The Soviet Foreign Minister, Vyacheslav Molotov, announced that none of the Germans captured in Stalingrad would be set free until the city had been rebuilt.

So useful did the Soviets find the German soldiers as slave labour that they were kept at work long after the war ended. The last known German prisoner was repatriated in 1955. Rumours abounded for years that other German soldiers were kept in the gulags as late as 1967. Of the 111,465 Germans captured in Stalingrad, only 5,000 lived long enough to go home.

The fate of the leading characters

Of the individuals named in this book, most survived the fighting at Stalingrad long enough to record their experiences for posterity. Not all survived the war.

Adolf Hitler remained as dictator of Germany until he committed suicide in the ruins of Berlin on 30 April 1945. After Stalingrad he interfered more and more in the running of the war, with what are generally considered to have been disastrous results.

Stalin was the absolute ruler of the Soviet Union until his death on 5 March 1953. Once the war was won he became increasingly autocratic and launched vengeful campaigns against communities he believed had aided the invaders. He also imposed Communist rule, which effectively meant direct Soviet rule, on the countries of Eastern Europe.

After the failure of the *Luftwaffe* to supply the 6th Army at Stalingrad, Goering was in disgrace with Hitler. He retired from all but ceremonial duties for the rest of the war. At the Nuremberg Trials he was convicted of crimes against humanity and sentenced to death, but he committed suicide before his execution was carried out.

Field Marshal Paulus was well treated by the

Soviets, but he refused to admit that the Germans had committed war crimes, so he did not sign any of the papers put in front of him. Following the death of his son Friedrich, who died fighting in Italy, and the failure of the 20 July 1944 plot by German officers to kill Hitler, Paulus agreed to make broadcasts calling on the Germans to surrender. He was a witness for the prosecution at the Nuremberg Trials. Released in 1953, he retired to East Germany, where he died in 1957.

General Schmidt, Paulus's deputy, refused to help the Soviets in any way and was often rude and aggressive to his captors. He was released in 1955 and moved to West Germany, where he died in 1957.

General Manstein saw his Army Group Don take over Army Group B in March 1943. He continued to hold high command in the German army and fought a series of skilful actions until he was promoted to field marshal and removed from active command by Hitler, who had become annoyed at Manstein's retreats. In the War Crimes trials he was found guilty of failing to protect civilians from mistreatment and spent four years in prison. On his release he served with the West German government and played a major role in rebuilding the German army. He died in 1973.

Field Marshal von Weichs lost command of Army Group B to Manstein in March 1943 and became Commander of Army Group F in the Balkans. He later commanded the German retreat from the Balkans and was captured by the Americans. He was freed in 1947 and died in 1954.

Field Marshal von List lived in retirement after Hitler sacked him. At the Nuremberg Trials he was convicted of executing hostages and spent four years in prison. He died in 1971.

Field Marshal von Kleist continued to hold high command until March 1944 when he ordered a retreat that had been forbidden by Hitler. He was later captured by the Soviets and sentenced to ten years in prison for war crimes. He died in captivity in 1954.

Field Marshal von Bock was given no new commands after being sacked by Hitler. He was killed during an air raid just eight days before the end of the war, in May 1945.

The panzer general, Hermann Balck, continued to command panzers until he surrendered to the Americans on 8 May 1945. In 1947 he was found guilty of murder for having executed an officer in 1944 without trial. He was soon released and lived until 1982.

Panzer general Hermann Hoth was sacked by Hitler in 1943 after he suffered a setback. He lived in retirement until he was sent to prison for ten years following the Nuremberg Trials. He was released in 1954 and over the next 15 years he wrote a number of highly regarded books on military history. He died in 1971.

Another panzer commander, General Hans-Valentin Hube, 'The Man', continued to command panzers until he was killed in an air crash in 1944.

Romanian leader Ion Antonescu was toppled from power in early 1944 by King Michael of Romania. In 1946 he was found guilty of war crimes and executed.

Soviet General Vasily Chuikov commanded the 62nd Army in Stalingrad. After Stalingrad, the 62nd Army was redesignated the 8th Guards Army. Chuikov led that army all the way to Berlin. After the war he was made a Marshal of the Soviet Union and in 1962 he became Commander-in-Chief of the entire Red Army. He retired in 1972 and died in 1982.

General Georgy Zhukov continued to hold high command in the Red Army until the end of the war and was present when the Germans surrendered after the death of Hitler. Stalin considered Zhukov to be too popular and influential, so he sacked him in 1946. After Stalin's death Zhukov was reinstated and made Defence Minister. He retired in 1957, published an autobiography in 1969 and died in 1974.

General Konstantin Rokossovsky continued to command Soviet armies until the end of the war and it was his troops who linked up with those of the British in northern Germany in 1945.

He then returned to his native Poland to become head of the Polish armed forces. In 1957 he went back to Russia as Chief Inspector of the Red Army. He retired in 1962 and died in 1968.

General Andrey Yeremenko led the Soviet forces into the Balkans in 1944 and 1945. He held a number of senior commands after 1945 and in 1955 was raised to the rank of Marshal. He retired in 1958 and died in 1970.

After being superseded by Zhukov, Semyon Timoshenko held a succession of unimportant commands. He retired from the Red Army in 1961 and died in 1970.

General Filipp Golikov was moved to the Ministry of Defence after the war and held a number of relatively junior positions until his retirement. He died in 1980.

Soviet sniper Vasily Zaytsev was later allowed to return to the front line. Despite being wounded he remained in action until 1943, when he received an injury that affected his eyesight. He was awarded the title Hero of the Soviet Union and was credited with a total of 225 kills. After the war he qualified as a textile engineer and moved to Kiev, where he rose to be director of a clothing factory. He died in 1991, aged 76.

Yakov Pavlov, who commanded operations at

Pavlov's House, was awarded the title Hero of the Soviet Union, the Order of Lenin, the Order of the October Revolution, two Orders of the Red Star and numerous other medals. He served three terms in the Supreme Soviet of the Russian Soviet Federative Socialist Republic. Pavlov died in 1981.

As for the 6th Army, it had died at Stalingrad, but it was to be reborn. That was why Hitler had wanted one man from each division flown out at the last minute. Based on those single men, each division was reformed exactly as it had been before Stalingrad. The new 6th Army became active on 5 March 1943. It fought on the Eastern Front until its cohesion and command structure was smashed by a Soviet offensive in March 1945. Most of the survivors then fled west as quickly as possible, so that they could surrender to the Americans. The army officially ceased to exist on 9 May 1945, when its then commander, Hermann Balck, surrendered himself and his remaining men to the Americans near Vienna.

MAIN PLAYERS

POLITICIANS

Germany

Adolf Hitler, Chancellor

Joachim von Ribbentrop, Foreign Minister

Josef Goebbels, Propaganda Chief

Hermann Goering, Head of the Luftwaffe

Soviet Union

Josef Stalin, Premier

Vyacheslav Molotov, Foreign Minister

Lavrentiy Beria, Head of State Security

Georgy Malenkov, Head of the State Defence Committee

Nikita Khrushchev, Head of Civil Administration, Stalingrad

Hungary

Admiral Miklós Horthy, Ruler

Romania

Ignacy Mosciki, President

Slovak State

Jozef Tiso, Head of State

MILITARY FORCES

Germany

Field Marshal Wilhelm Keitel, Supreme Commander (OKW)

Field Marshal Walther von Brauchitsch, Commander-in-Chief of
the German Army

Field Marshall Wilhelm von Leeb, Commander Army Group
North

Field Marshal Georg von Küchler, Commander Army Group
North

Field Marshal Fedor von Bock, Commander Army Group
Centre

Field Marshal Gerd von Rundstedt, Commander Army Group
South

Field Marshal Wilhelm von List, Commander Army Group A
Southern

Field Marshal Maximilian von Weichs, Commander Army
Group B Northern

Field Marshal Erich von Manstein, Commander 11th Army

Field Marshal Walther von Reichenau, Commander 6th Army

Field Marshal Wolfram Freiherr von Richthofen, Head of
Tactical and Operational Support, Luftwaffe

General Alfred Jodl, Head of Operations Staff (OKW)

General Franz Halder, Head of General Staff (OKH)

General Kurt Zeitzler, Head of General Staff (OKH)

General Günther Blumentritt, Head of Supplies and Transport (OKH)

General Walter Warlimont, Deputy Head of Operations Staff

General (then Field Marshal) Ewald von Kleist, Commander 1st Panzer Corp (then Commander Army Group A)

General (then Field Marshal) Friedrich Paulus, Commander 6th Army

General Carl-Heinrich von Stülpnagel, Commander 17th Army

General Richard Ruoff, Commander 17th Army

General Arthur Schmidt, Chief of Staff 6th Army

General Franz Landgraf, Commander 6th Panzer Division

General Hermann Balck, Commander 11th Panzer Division

General Hans-Georg Leyser, Commander 29th Panzergrenadier Division

General Walter Graf von Brockdorff-Ahlefeldt, Commander SS Division *Totenkopf*

General Hermann Hoth, Commander 3rd Panzer Group

General Heinz Guderian, Commander 2nd Panzer Group

General Erich Hoepner, Commander 4th Panzer Group

General Ferdinand Heim, Commander 48th Panzer Corps

General Eberhard von Mackensen, Commander 1st Panzer Corps

General Gustav von Wietersheim, Commander 14th Panzer
    Corps

General Hans-Valentin Hube, Commander 14th Panzer Corps

General Karl-Adolf Hollidt, Commander 17th Army Corps

General Viktor von Schwedler, Commander 4th Panzer Corps

General Walther von Seydlitz, Commander 51st Army Corps

General Jans Jeschonnek, Chief of the General Staff, Luftwaffe

General Rudolf Schmundt, Head of Army Personnel
    Department

Soviet Union

Marshal Aleksandr Vasilevsky, Chief of General Staff

Marshal Georgy Zhukov, Chief of General Staff

Marshal Semyon Timoshenko, Commander Western Front

Marshal Andrey Yeremenko, Commander Western Front

Marshal Semyon Budenny, Commander Southern Front

Marshal Rodion Malinovsky, Commander Southern Front

Marshal Kirill Meretskov, Commander Volkhov Front

General Ivan Petrov, Commander Southern Front

General Filipp Golikov, Chief of Intelligence, Deputy
    Commander Southwest Front

General Andrei Vlasov, Commander 2nd Shock Army

General Konstantin Rokossovsky, Commander 16th Army

General Vasily Chuikov, Commander 64th Army

General Aleksandr Rodimtsev, Commander 13th Guards
Division

General Viktor Zholudev, Commander 37th Guards Division

Lieutenant General Dmitry Kozlov, Commander Caucasian
Front

Lieutenant-General Konstantin Golubev, Commander 43rd
Army

Colonel Aleksandr Sarayev, Head of NKVD Stalingrad

Colonel Leonid Gurtiev, Commander 308th Rifle Division

Captain Vassily Yeroshenko, Tashkent Commander

Romania

Marshal Ion Antonescu, Commander-in-Chief Land Forces

General Petre Dumitrescu, Commander 3rd Army

General Mihail Lascar, 1st Mounted Brigade

PICTURE CREDITS

Plate page 1
Top   Bild 101I-771-0366-02A o.Ang.
Bottom   Bild 101I-163-0319-07A Bauer

Plate page 2
Top   Bild 101I-056-1643-29A Harren
Bottom   Bild 146-1975-081-21 Weidner

Plate page 3
Top   Bild 101I-138-1068-06 Dreyer
Bottom left   RIA Novosti
Bottom right   Bild 183-L29871 Hermann

Plate page 4
Top   RIA Novosti
Bottom   RIA Novosti

Plate page 5
Top left   RIA Novosti
Top right   RIA Novosti
Bottom left   Bild 183-B12867 Gutjahr
Bottom right   RIA Novosti

Plate page 6
Top   RIA Novosti
Centre   Bild 183-B22176 o.Ang.
Bottom   RIA Novosti

Plate page 7

Top	RIA Novosti
Centre	RIA Novosti
Bottom left	Bild 146-1991-015-31A Mittelstaedt, Heinz
Bottom right	Bild 146-1971-070-73 Jesse

Plate page 8

Top	RIA Novosti
Centre left	RIA Novosti
Centre right	RIA Novosti
Bottom	RIA Novosti